Henry Tyrer, 1858–1936, Founder and Governing Director

HENRY TYRER

A Liverpool Shipping Agent
and His Enterprise, 1879–1979

HENRY TYRER

A LIVERPOOL SHIPPING AGENT
AND HIS ENTERPRISE, 1879–1979

PETER N. DAVIES

CROOM HELM LONDON

© 1979 Peter N. Davies
Croom Helm Ltd, 2-10 St John's Road, London SW11

British Library Cataloguing in Publication Data
Davies, Peter Neville
    Henry Tyrer.
    1. Henry Tyrer and Company — History
    387.5'1   HE610.G7
    ISBN 0–85664–966–X

TO SIMON

Typeset by Leaper & Gard Limited, Bristol
Printed and bound in Great Britain
REDWOOD BURN LIMITED
Trowbridge & Esher

CONTENTS

FOREWORD

A century of trading by a private company is no mean achievement in any major field of commercial activity. This is especially true within the shipping industry and its ancillary services for competition in these spheres has traditionally been extremely keen. As a result, many of the smaller operators have succumbed to the giants of their trade and have either lost their identities completely or, while retaining their original names, merely carry out the policies laid down by others. In turn, this has led to the demise of the individualistic touch which previously characterised many businesses and to its replacement by a standardised conformity.

In these circumstances the survival of Henry Tyrer & Company Ltd, for a period of 100 years is in itself a major reason for recording its formation and subsequent progress. In addition, the facts of this particular case tell the extraordinary story of how a farmer's son, without any advantages beyond those supplied by a moderate education and a happy family background, was able to build a highly successful and long-lived enterprise.

As the third son Henry Tyrer saw no future in remaining at home to toil on the land, he thought fit at an early age to look in other directions to earn a living. The relative nearness of Liverpool provided an irresistible attraction and Henry secured a job which involved long hours but only meagre pay. Then, by saving hard and learning well, he was able, while still a very young man, to open up on his own account as a commission merchant in the West African trade.

This venture placed Henry Tyrer in direct competition with many established firms but although he received many set-backs his determination never faltered. This characteristic was an important factor in ensuring the viability of the business during Tyrer's lifetime, and both Thomas Wilson and Frederick Cutts — the second and third Chairman respectively — were well indoctrinated in this respect. I, as the fourth Chairman must also confess to have been greatly influenced by the ideas and customs that I inherited from such predecessors. Since joining Tyrers' at the age of 15 I have served under several hard 'task masters'. My apprenticeship continued right up to the time I was granted a seat on the Board in 1956 and, on many occasions since, I have been grateful for the rigorous training I received. When I joined the firm in 1935 Henry Tyrer was no longer in real control but he treated me in a kindly way and I absorbed a little of his attitudes and methods. Thomas Wilson who followed in Tyrer's position and was very much in his mould re-inforced these lessons but as he was Chairman and I a very junior clerk we operated on very different wave-bands.

With Frederick Cutts, the position gradually changed for, although he had already been with the Company for 38 years when I became a member he was to remain with Tyrers' for a further 34 years. During this time I advanced from my first lowly position to that of Vice Chairman and I got to know my senior extremely well. This is not to suggest that we always agreed but our differences such as they were, were never personal but invariably concerned with the good of the Company. Mr Cutts, without doubt, taught me a great deal and I would like to acknowledge publicly the immense debt that I owe him. My other mentor and, I may say, friend, was and still is Mr R.L. Jones. As the 'Guiding Light' of Freight Conveyors Mr Jones was able to provide an additional dimension to my training and later when I became Chairman I was always happy to listen to his advice. He is now the oldest surviving member of the 'Old School' and still takes great delight in its progress and prosperity. To him I would wish to convey my gratitude for all his past efforts and hope that his present retirement may continue to be a long and pleasant one.

Today the Company which Henry Tyrer founded so long ago has risen from its humble origins to become a prominent and well respected member of the Shipping Fraternity in Liverpool. The esteem in which the Company is held is reflected in the fact that the Liverpool Steam Ship Owners Association has seen fit to invite me to be its Chairman for 1979/80 which I take to be a great honour attaching to the Company. The Company however is not resting on its laurels even in this centenary year but is ever watchful for new opportunities to expand and diversify, following the tradition set by Henry Tyrer himself.

It should not be forgotten that governing Directors and Chairmen seldom achieve anything by themselves and I am most conscious of the debt that I personally owe to the present Board. Each and every member has given me his unstinted support and so deserves my grateful thanks. In turn, the Directors cannot work in isolation so I wish to pay tribute also to all those employees past and present and at every level who have contributed in their various ways to the success of the Company. In a trade such as ours where we depend more on the services of people than machines, it is vitally important that we can count on their reliability and loyalty and in this respect we have been in the past and

Foreword

are today extremely fortunate.

    Finally, I would like to express my sincere thanks to the Author for the production of this history. It was my good fortune to have met Peter Davies when he visited Mr Cutts for regular discussions in respect of the West African trade. It seemed appropriate therefore to consult him when the current study was proposed and I was especially pleased when he agreed to undertake the task himself. During the past two years our mutual understanding and respect have continued to develop and I am now happy to regard him as a friend as well as a scholar who has helped to place the achievements of Henry Tyrer and his Company in true perspective. Dr Davies has undertaken extensive research in the compilation of this work which has revealed much interesting information and thrown light on some chapters of our history of which little was previously known. It does much to reflect the changed nature of the Liverpool shipping scene over the years and is a most informative and readable study which I feel sure will commend itself to all who have an interest in the shipping industry in general and in particular, Liverpool's maritime history.

December 1978   Charles W. Harrison
Liverpool   Chairman
Henry Tyrer & Company Limited

PREFACE

My first connection with Henry Tyrer and Company was in the early 1960s when I was engaged in research into the life of Sir Alfred Jones.[1] This brought me in touch with Frederick Cutts and Charles Harrison but in the beginning very little of value emerged from our conversations. It eventually transpired that Mr Cutts was constrained by two distinct motives. He mistakenly believed that Henry Tyrer had been declared bankrupt in his early days[2] and was anxious not to say anything that showed his 'old governor' in a poor light. He also felt that he was under an obligation not to disclose any of his firm's former relationships with the United Africa Company. This feeling was so strong that it could only be ended by the personal intervention of Lord Cole, then Chairman of Unilever, when — several years later — I was undertaking a further investigation into the West African Shipping trade.[3]

Thereafter Mr Cutts proved to be extremely helpful and with an experience of the business which dated back to 1897 he was able to use his first-hand knowledge to shed light on many of the problems which I had encountered. In addition to aiding my understanding of West African commerce, Mr Cutts explained in some detail the role of Henry Tyrer and his firm and also introduced me to Mr W.K. Findlay with whom Tyrer's had established links in 1903.[4]

William Findlay had been born in Angus in 1868 and went out to West Africa in 1889 on behalf of the merchanting firm of W.B. MacIver and Company. He subsequently purchased this concern and after re-selling it to Lever's in 1910 he became closely associated with Mr W.H. Lever. For many years, thereafter, he served as a director of Lever Brothers and, as well as being Managing Director of the Bromport Steamship Company, acted as Chairman of the Niger Company until he retired in 1931.

In 1965 Mr Findlay saw a picture of Frederick Cutts in the *Liverpool Echo*. He remembered that Henry Tyrer and Company had been the firm which arranged for *Prestonian* to visit West Africa for MacIver's in 1903 and 1904 and decided to renew their friendship.[5] He then wrote to Mr Cutts and thus began a correspondence which was to prove of great interest to both men.

Mr Cutts then suggested that I should meet his old acquaintance and this took place at Tyrer's office in Vernon Street, Liverpool, in July

1965. Mr Findlay was then aged 97 and Mr Cutts was in his 85th year and the two men had not met for at least thirty five years. The ensuing discussion was fascinating and covered many aspects of the West African trade so that when it was over I felt both better informed and highly privileged.

By this time I had met Charles Harrison on several occasions but then the contact was broken and it was not until 1976 that we met again. Mr Harrison then informed me that Tyrer's were approaching their centenary and asked if I could recommend an author who could write a suitable history. It so happened that in the intervening period my own work had been almost entirely concerned with West African shipping and trading[6] so it was not long before it was mutually determined that I should undertake the task myself.

During the past two years I have learned an enormous amount about Henry Tyrer and Company and found that what I had regarded as a relatively small project was, in fact, of substantial proportions. My expertise in West African affairs proved to be only a useful foundation for what turned out to be an extensive business with multifarious aspects and, in consequence, I found myself involved with many fresh areas of commerce. Fortunately the four chairmen of the Company provided a common thread so its development may conveniently be seen through the activities organised in turn by Henry Tyrer, Thomas Wilson, Frederick Cutts and Charles Harrison. The recent diversification into new fields of endeavour has meant, in practice, that the firm has virtually been re-born during the past decade so it would seem that Henry Tyrer's spirit of enterprise lives on within the present management.

Throughout my research I have been given every possible help by the firm's current directors. To these I offer my sincere thanks and would particularly like to mention Tyrer's former Vice-Chairman, Mr J.E. Lyons, who generously gave of his time so that my understanding would be more complete. Mr G.B. Hannan assisted with the references to the Bugsier and CNAN agencies, while Mr D.C. Harrison and Mr R. Kaye provided the background to Ben Line Containers and to Tyrer's involvement in the timber trade. They also explained in some detail the way in which Tyrer Transport Services came into being. Mr J. Lea, at present operations director, made his long experience available to me at all times and proved to be a most valuable source of what were, sometimes, obscure details. Mr J.F. Sanders who is now responsible for the Indian trade, guided me to a better appreciation of agency relationships and Mr G.E. Stretch, currently in charge of all disbursement accounts, helped to explain the working of the whaling industry.

My gratitude is also due to Messrs K. Dalzell and N.C. Harris for their assistance with the references to Preston Office, to Mr B. Dowd — the Company Secretary — for his complete co-operation at all times, to Mr R.L. Jones for his help in respect of Freight Conveyors and to Mr D. Ollerton for information particularly regarding the Southern Scotland Service. In addition, Mr A. Caster (Port of Preston, Dock Office), Mrs Maud Harrison (niece of Henry Tyrer), John Hothersall Junior (Joseph Pyke and Son), Gordon Jackson (of Strathclyde University) and Mr P.J. Sutcliffe (of the Mersey Dock and Harbour Company) have all contributed in their own ways and deserve my grateful appreciation. Furthermore, I would like to pay a special tribute to Mr H.A. Fair of Messrs Warlow and Fair, the Company's Auditors. His aid in interpreting the Company's performance has been invaluable and he deserves my sincere thanks.

Finally, I must acknowledge my enormous debt to Charles Harrison for his patience, understanding and friendship. He has undoubtedly lightened my burden by every means within his power without, at any state, attempting to prevent the production of an objective analysis. Consequently, while this work provides what is intended to be a readable account of Tyrer's first one hundred years in business, it is hoped that it also supplies one of the first serious studies of a successful small entrepreneur and of his enterprise.

University of Liverpool   P.N. Davies
November 1978

Notes

1. 'Sir Alfred Jones and the Development of West African Trade', MA thesis, University of Liverpool, 1964.
2. See below, Chapter 2, pp. 31-3.
3. 'British Shipping and the Growth of the West African Economy', 1910-50, PhD thesis, University of Liverpool, 1967.
4. See below, Chapter 3, pp. 45-6.
5. Ibid.
6. P.N. Davies, *The Trade Makers: Elder Dempster in West Africa, 1852-1972* (George Allen and Unwin, London, 1972); *Trading in West Africa* (ed.) (Croom Helm, London, 1976); *Sir Alfred Jones: Shipping Entrepreneur par Excellence* (Europa Library of Business Biography, London, 1978).

1 THE EARLY LIFE OF HENRY TYRER

I

The village of Burscough where Henry Tyrer spent his early life and in which vicinity his ancestors had reputedly farmed for many generations is situated in south-west Lancashire about three miles from the ancient town of Ormskirk. The name suggests a Norse origin and it is probable that the area was occupied by Viking invaders during the ninth or tenth centuries. It seems certain that farming has been continued without interruption since at least Norman times and agriculture still remains the main source of local employment.

In the mid-nineteenth century, the population numbered less than two thousand but, although the traditional way of life was little changed, the advent of the Leeds and Liverpool Canal[1] had brought Burscough into closer touch with the outside world. The building of the railway[2] between Liverpool and Preston in 1849 further continued this process for a station was constructed at Burscough Junction. This had the effect of encouraging the growing of cash crops, and sales of fresh vegetables were added to the customary production of wheat, oats and potatoes. It also resulted in the beginning of rural settlement by a new breed of men who utilised the frequent train services to commute to their employment in the nearby towns and cities.

This growth of population, together with the obvious potential of the area, led the ecclesiastical authorities to form a new parish in 1847. This included the two villages of Burscough and Burscough Bridge together with part of Lathom and was based on the Anglican church of St John which had been completed in 1832 and which could seat nearly a thousand people. The parish also contained a much smaller Catholic church as well as Wesleyan and Primitive Methodist chapels and the ruins of the ancient priory of St Nicholas.[3] The two villages included a post office, a doctor's surgery, several schools, a number of inns and public houses and a variety of shops which could provide everything necessary to maintain a simple standard of living. Many services and trades were also available. These all reflected the agricultural interests of the parish and all were on a very small scale except for a firm of 'steam corn millers', a brickworks and two companies of 'wholesale potato, fruit, seed and manure merchants'.

In spite of this limited development, however, Burscough remained a tiny rural community where life proceeded at a slow and sedate pace. The principal landowner and lord of the manor was the Earl of Derby but in view of his enormous estates and residence elsewhere it is doubtful if he ever paid more than the briefest of visits to his holdings in the district. Burscough did, of course, possess some gentle folk but most of its inhabitants had to earn their own living and a substantial number were farmers of one kind or another.

Amongst this latter group was a certain Cuthbert Tyrer whose ancestors had reputedly farmed in the region for many generations. Also farming in Burscough at this time was John Travis and the two families were united when in December 1843, their respective son and daughter, John Tyrer and Jane Travis, were married in Ormskirk Parish Church. Their union eventually resulted in the birth of no fewer than thirteen children. Unfortunately only seven of these were to live to maturity but the survivors included Henry, the third son, who was born on 2 March 1858.[4]

II

Henry Tyrer first saw the light of day at Green Lane Farm, Ormskirk, but spent most of his early life at Manor House Farm, which was situated at the end of High Lane in Burscough.[5] Here he developed a love of the soil and an interest in country pursuits that was to stay with him for the rest of his life. As a member of a large family he can hardly have been 'spoilt' by his parents but, nevertheless, within the constraints of a limited budget he was indulged to a modest degree. Thus he was able to attempt the breeding and training of 'homing' pigeons from quite an early age but on a working farm all had to contribute as much as possible and little time was available for even the most rewarding of hobbies.

Although there were a number of schools in Burscough and Burscough Bridge they were only intended to provide an elementary type of education. If Henry ever attended one of these establishments there is no record of it and it could only have been for a year or two at most: what is certain is that he was regarded as a bright and studious boy and it was decided, therefore, that he would benefit from attendance at the Free Grammar School in Ruff Lane, Ormskirk. This was an ancient institution, founded in 1614, which could accommodate approximately seventy pupils. In spite of its name, tuition fees of between £4 and £8 per year were charged[6] so Henry was fortunate both in having such an excellent school so near to his home and in possessing parents who were both willing and able to pay for his instruction.

Henry was a pupil at the Grammar School from the mid 1860s to 1872 and he followed the normal curriculum of the day concentrating on the Classics, English and Mathematics. It was during this period that he developed a strong love of sport – an interest which subsequently resulted in a life-long attachment to cricket, golf and bowls. No evidence has survived to indicate why Henry chose to leave at the age of fourteen[7] but it is probable that by then he had decided to seek a career in business and had come to the conclusion that an early start would be of more use than further education. It also seems likely that the timing of his decision was influenced by the activities of his brothers who were all making progress in their various careers[8] and that he resented being the odd man out.

Henry undoubtedly realised that his education would be wasted if he stayed on the farm and understood that there was very little scope for other employment which offered hope of advancement if he remained at home. With two elder and one younger brother keen to stay on the land the family holdings were already inadequate and few other opportunities were available in Burscough. Ormskirk was, of course, much larger, having a population of nearly six thousand but, it too, could offer only limited prospects to an ambitious man. Clearly if Henry Tyrer wished to make a decisive mark in the world he would have to look further afield. In practical terms this meant that the growing port of Liverpool was an obvious first choice for in addition to its undoubted potential it also had the advantage of such excellent rail links that Henry could continue to live at home.

III

Liverpool first came into prominence in 1207 when King John, seeking an additional base for his proposed operations against Ireland, granted a charter which established it as a royal borough. Thereafter progress was slow and it was not until 1660 that the port was finally recognised as being legally separate and distinct from Chester. By then trade based on 'Lancashire coals and cotton goods and Cheshire salt and cheese'[9] was growing to a significant size and was being encouraged by large imports of tobacco from Virginia and sugar from the West Indies.

After 1700 Liverpool became important in the 'Triangular Trade' in which manufactured goods from the Midlands and cottons from Manchester were exchanged for slaves on the west coast of Africa. In turn, the slaves were sold in the West Indies or Southern States of America and then the vessels returned home with cargoes of rum, cotton and sugar when these were available.[10] In time Liverpool replaced both

London and Bristol and became the leading port in this trade, partly because of the ease with which exports could be purchased and partly because of the local demand for the items being imported. In addition, the building of the first wet dock in 1715 gave Liverpool a considerable competitive advantage over its rivals and this was consolidated when a second wet dock was constructed in 1753. By then salt was a major export, cargoes being sent to Newfoundland for use by the fishing industry and being exchanged for wine and fruit in many Mediterranean countries, so the new facility was quite appropriately named as 'Salthouse' dock.

The growth of industry in Lancashire and Yorkshire which goes under the title of 'The Industrial Revolution' and which reached its peak in the years between 1760 and 1820 had obvious repercussions for Liverpool. It became the major channel by which food and raw materials could be brought into this expanding sector of the British economy and provided by far the most important outlet for its manufactured goods and its coal. This process was greatly assisted by the building of a canal system which connected the docks to their hinterland,[11] and was further encouraged by what was really the world's first railway network.[12]

A vital consequence of these enhanced activities was that shipping services, already important, were extended to all parts of the world.[13] These developments were subsequently strengthened by the replacement of sail by steam and of wood by iron and then steel, for Liverpool was ideally placed to take advantage of these technological innovations. The growth of trade and of shipping then led to a further expansion of the port and by 1857 it possessed no less than twenty-one enclosed docks. They also resulted in Merseyside becoming the nation's second most important shipping centre (after London) and thus the city became one of the world's most dynamic commercial entities.

The employment opportunities available because of Liverpool's economic development led to a dramatic growth of its population. This had amounted to approximately 77,000 in 1801 but by the 1870s it had risen to over half a million.[14] By then the pace of increase was beginning to slacken but, even so, by 1911 the Merseyside conurbation had over one million people living within its boundaries — Liverpool's share amounting to nearly 750,000.[15]

A majority of the growing population resulted from the natural increase of the indigenous inhabitants but migration was extremely important, particularly in the period up to 1861. At that date immigrants made up 49 per cent of Liverpool's citizens — about half of these having originated from Ireland.[16] By 1911 the proportion of immigrants had declined to only 24 per cent[17] and the Irish component was only 5 per cent of the total population. The remainder included many families from Scotland and North Wales and also a large number from all over England. Amongst the latter were many from Lancashire itself and, in addition, where communications were suitable many 'local' people chose to commute from outside the city's boundaries.

IV

Henry Tyrer's decision to seek fame and fortune in Liverpool was easily translated into action. It took a bare thirty minutes for him to travel by train to Exchange station which was conveniently situated for the city's commercial sector. Once on Merseyside, however, there can be little doubt that he must have spent many weary hours searching for suitable employment for although the port was a hive of activity there were numerous applicants for each vacancy. Eventually it seems that Henry decided that he must follow in the footsteps of such successful 'immigrants' as Alexander Elder, John Dempster,[18] John Holt[19] and Alfred Jones[20] and towards the end of 1872 he entered the West African trade by securing a position with James Murdoch and Company of Rumford Place.

Liverpool's connection with the west coast of Africa dated back to its involvement in the slave trade. When this was abolished in 1807 it led to a considerable decline in activity. Gradually, however, trade in palm oil, palm kernels and other 'legitimate' items increased and this development received an important boost when the African Steam Ship Company began to operate a series of regular sailings in 1853.[21] At first this operated from London but, in 1856, Liverpool was made the UK terminal of the line and this ensured that the trade was firmly and finally centred on Merseyside. A second firm, the British and African Steam Navigation Company, did commence a service from Glasgow in 1869 but by 1874 this direct link had been discontinued and, thereafter, all of its sailings either called at, or originated from Liverpool.

Palm oil and palm kernels continued to provide the chief exports of British West Africa after regular steam-shipping services had been introduced and in the period from 1854 to 1913 they formed between 43% to 76% of annual totals.[22] This was because of two main factors: it was necessary to import more and more quantities of edible oils and fats just to maintain existing standards at a time when the population of the United Kingdom was rapidly rising; it was also found that additional quantities of these and similar items were needed to satisfy the growing market for soap and candles and this trend was further strengthened when, later in the century, it was discovered that palm kernel oil possessed valuable keeping qualities and was therefore extremely useful for the manufacture of margarine.

The consequence of this demand was that an average of 50,000 tons per year were exported from the coast and this provided the basis for the very successful shipping businesses operated by the two British lines. It also formed the raison d'être of many ancillary companies and partnerships such as commission and general agents, insurance and shipping brokers, coopers, packers and, of course, numerous varieties and sizes of firms of merchants.

V

James Murdoch and Company, whom Henry Tyrer was to join in 1872, had its origins in the partnership of James Murdoch and David L. Murdoch which began to trade in 1847. At that date they were described as 'Shipbrokers and Commission Agents' and occupied offices at Brazilian Buildings, 14 Drury Lane, in the centre of the city.[23] The following year the firm had moved to 76 South Castle Street and David L. Murdoch was listed as a 'Shipbroker' and James Murdoch as a 'Cornbroker and Commission Agent'.[24]

Nothing further is known of the antecedents of the Company except that in 1849 it acquired the agency of the Standard Life Assurance.[25] The partnership then appears to have been dissolved, either by death or mutual consent, and there is no further mention of David L. Murdoch. His former partner, however, appears in the records for 1851 as James Murdoch and Company, Commission Agents, with offices at 15 Rumford Street.[26] Two years later his premises are shown as 12 Rumford Place, and here he was to remain until he retired some twenty-seven years later.

In 1855 James Murdoch was shown as a partner in the firm of C.S. Middleton and Son who were merchants with offices also at 12 Rumford Place. This appears to have been a shortlived affair and there is no second mention of Murdoch in connection with this business. Instead he seems to have worked alone for a five year period but then, in 1860, he was joined by Frederick Grant and their partnership became known as 'Grant, Murdoch and Company, Merchants and Shipowners'.[27] An interesting point to note here is that both James Murdoch and Frederick Grant are described as living in 'Gorst Hills', Sutton, Cheshire,[28] so perhaps this formed part of the bond which drew them together. Also of interest is the fact that although their business association was only to last a few years their firm was always subsequently referred to as 'Grant, Murdoch and Company'.[29]

By 1868 Frederick Grant had left and Murdoch had taken a new partner. He was Thomas Pain of Birkenhead and they operated under the name of 'Murdoch, Pain and Company, General Merchants'.[30] This association also had but a brief existence and by 1872 Murdoch was again on his own. It appears, however, that the retirement of Thomas Pain did not affect the viability of the concern for soon after his departure James Murdoch was appointed as agent for Jules, Robin and Company of Cognac[31] and in 1874 found it necessary to purchase (or lease) a cooperage at 74 and 76 Norfolk Street.[32] The loss of a partner plus the expansion of the business thus provided the need for additional staff and Henry Tyrer was enabled to secure his first employment.

VI

Henry Tyrer was still only fourteen years of age when he joined James Murdoch and Company so, as might be expected, his duties were of a very modest nature. The firm still retained its offices in Rumford Place and its cooperage in Norfolk Street but Tyrer spent most of his early days working outside '. . . for three years he practically lived on the George dock, supervising the loading and unloading, and dispatch of ships . . .'[33]

Following this period of apprenticeship Tyrer spent more and more time in the cooperage which was a vital part of Murdoch's West African trade. Palm oil needed to be transported in casks and it was customary for West African merchants to provide these for their agents and clients. In most cases the staves, tops and bottoms were purchased but then had to be assembled to form a liquid-tight barrel. To save freight charges the cask would then be broken down to form a shook – the component staves being packed into the smallest possible bundle – and would be shipped in that form to the Niger Delta. There the shook would be put together again and the resulting container used for the carriage of the oil. At that time many casks would be used again and again so the Liverpool cooperage would be required to inspect and repair these items as well as deal with the new ones. Murdoch's agency for brandy imported from Cognac would also have provided some additional work for this side of the firm's activities.

Having mastered the elementary and technical aspects of his trade Tyrer was then initiated into the mysteries of buying and selling and, as he gained a comprehensive picture of the firm's activities, began to appreciate the true potential of the business. It seems that Tyrer proved to be an apt pupil and Murdoch gave him progressively larger responsibilities. This development was certain to be encouraged by James Murdoch's advancing age for after some thirty years in business he was, without question, seeking a quieter life. Thus he groomed young Henry and, in 1879, accepted his twenty-one year old assistant as a partner into what then became known as Murdoch, Tyrer and Company.[34]

The terms of this partnership are not known but it is probable that they followed the normal custom of the day. This meant that Tyrer would only start with a small holding in the firm, perhaps 10 per cent, but that he would have the right to purchase further shares each year out of his proportion of the net profits. This, of course, meant that it would be many years before Tyrer could control the firm and still more years before he would own it completely. Whether this was of real significance or whether he had a basic disagreement with Murdoch cannot now be established — the only certainty is that soon after the partnership was formed, Henry Tyrer decided to form his own company.

Notes

1. Charles Hadfield and Gordon Biddle, *The Canals of North West England* (David and Charles, Newton Abbot, 1970), vol. 1, pp. 60-79.

2. John Marshall, *The Lancashire and Yorkshire Railway* (David and Charles, Newton Abbot, 1969), vol. 1, pp. 135-8.

3. A.N. Webb, *An Edition of the Cartulary of Burscough Priory*; printed for the Chetham Society (Manchester UP, 1970).

4. See Appendix Table 1, p. 137, for details of Tyrer's family tree.

5. *Ormskirk Advertiser*, 25 June 1936, Obituary of Henry Tyrer.

6. *Kelly's Lancashire Directory*, 1854.

7. The archives of Ormskirk Grammar School are now held at the Lancashire Record Office, Preston, but there is no mention of Henry Tyrer.

8. William and John became farmers; Robert became a provision dealer, but also retained an interest in farming.

9. G. Chandler, *Liverpool Shipping, a Short History* (Phoenix House, London, 1960), p. 22.

10. If cargoes were not available many ships returned home in ballast bringing the proceeds of their sales home in the form of Bills of Exchange.

11. Charles Hadfield, *British Canals* (Phoenix House, London, 1950), pp. 79-91, 134.

12. Marshall, *Lancashire and Yorkshire Railway*; J.A. Patmore and J. Clarke, *Railway History in Pictures, North-West England* (David and Charles, Newton Abbot, 1968), p. 6.

13. Francis E. Hyde, *Liverpool and the Mersey* (David and Charles, Newton Abbot, 1971), pp. 95-114.

14. This is taking the combined figures for Liverpool and the West Derby Hundred which covered most of the surrounding area.

15. R. Lawton, 'Genesis of Population', in *Merseyside: A Scientific Survey*, published for the British Association (University Press, Liverpool, 1953), p. 128.

16. Ibid., p. 125.

17. Ibid., p. 128.

18. P.N. Davies, *The Trade Makers: Elder Dempster in West Africa, 1852-1972* (George Allen and Unwin, London, 1973), pp. 53-4.

19. Ibid., pp. 54-5. See also *Merchant Adventure* (John Holt and Company [Liverpool] Limited).

20. Ibid., pp. 73-91. See also P.N. Davies, *Sir Alfred Jones, Shipping Entrepreneur Par Excellence* (Europa, London, 1978).

21. P.N. Davies, *The African Steam Ship Company, Liverpool and Merseyside*, J.R. Harris (ed.), (London, Frank Cass and Company, 1969).

22. See Appendix Table 2, p. 138, for details of exports from British West Africa to the United Kingdom, 1854-1913.

23. Gores' *Liverpool Directory*, 1847.

24. Ibid., 1848.

25. Ibid., 1849.

26. Ibid., 1851.

27. Ibid., 1860.

28. Ibid.

29. *Shipping*, 'Shipping Sidelights', 1 April 1895, p. 534 and *Ormskirk Advertiser*, 'A Lathom Golden Wedding', 20 June 1935.

30. Gores' *Liverpool Directory*, 1868.

31. Ibid., 1873.

32. Ibid., 1874.

33. *Ormskirk Advertiser*, 'A Lathom Golden Wedding', 20 June 1935.

34. Gores' *Liverpool Directory*, 1880.

2

HENRY TYRER AND COMPANY

I

Once Henry Tyrer had made a definite decision to end his association with James Murdoch he approached Heywood's Bank[1] in Brunswick Street, Liverpool, and on 14 July 1879, opened an account in the name of Henry Tyrer and Company.[2] The new firm was to operate as 'ship-brokers and commission merchants' and Tyrer was described as the sole partner although James Lyon was later given authority to endorse all cheques.[3] Premises were quickly acquired at Baltic Buildings in Red Cross Street[4] but were subsequently relinquished in favour of more convenient offices at 8a Rumford Place.

The new accommodation was, of course, very close to that occupied by Tyrer's former partner at 12 Rumford Place. This may have just been a coincidence but when it is noted that 'Murdoch, Tyrer and Company' continued to trade for at least a further twelve months it suggests that some form of compromise may have been reached.[5] An additional shred of evidence to support this view is that Tyrer appears to have taken over the cooperage which Murdoch had operated in Norfolk Street since 1874.[6]

One possible explanation of these events assumes that James Murdoch was anxious to retire fairly quickly. In this case he might have made a second agreement with Henry Tyrer which, while not so advantageous as having a vigorous junior partner, would have enabled him to scale down the size of his business and dispose of its assets. This possibility is given credence by the subsequent removal of Murdoch's name from the commercial section of the local directory and by his complete absence from the residential pages.[7] Taken together this would certainly indicate that he terminated his business interests and either died, or left the district to enjoy his retirement elsewhere.

Whatever may be the truth which lies behind these suggestions there can be no doubt that Henry Tyrer quickly established his own independent firm on a viable basis. In the first instance this owed a great deal to his success as a 'Commission Merchant' for this was an aspect of commerce where Tyrer's youthful enthusiasm and ability to inspire confidence was sufficient to offset his limited financial resources. Little capital was, in fact, required for this activity as cash was usually received with each order. Tyrer's knowledge of the West African trade was especially valuable in this respect and by taking personal charge of every transaction, however small, he soon earned a reputation which ensured that the volume of orders steadily increased.

Tyrer's progress as a 'Commission Merchant' was not unique and, indeed, in the Liverpool of the 1880s was not even remarkable. Many other small firms or partnerships were following similar paths and like Tyrer were seeking to become firmly established. The disadvantage of the 'commission' business was that it was irregular and erratic so any company which wished to achieve permanence needed to find a broader base for its activities. Tyrer grasped this principle from the beginning and, as noted above, he quickly acquired the use, if not the ownership, of Murdoch's cooperage. This immediately gave him an advantage over competitors who did not possess such a facility for it enabled him to diversify into additional areas. One such logical development was in wines and spirits for this not only brought more work into the cooperage but also provided a basic necessity for the West African trade. Tyrer's organisation of this integrated network of activities then gave him a competitive edge over many of his rivals and he was able, therefore, to consolidate and expand while others were failing to survive.

II

Henry Tyrer's early success was to a large extent the consequence of his 'vigilance, alertness and business capacity',[8] but his personal qualities would have been of no avail without sufficient quantities of capital. While an employee of James Murdoch and Company he continued to live at Green Lane, Ormskirk with his parents so his expenses would have been quite reasonable. To offset this was the daily cost of the rail fare to Liverpool so it seems unlikely that Tyrer was able to save very much from what, at first, must have been rather meagre wages.

It also seems clear that John Tyrer, Henry's father, was in no position to make a substantial contribution. He was a working farmer of very modest means whose sole capital was tied up in his land. Of course he could have pledged or mortgaged his holdings to obtain finance but this appears to be a very remote possibility. Henry, as one of many children, had only a limited claim on his parents[9] and would have found it difficult to justify a major investment in what was really a speculative venture. Almost certainly, therefore, Henry neither sought nor received financial assistance from either his family or his friends and, in fact, entered into his business career with a total capital of just £100.

Even in 1879 £100 was not a large sum of money and would have been quite inadequate to finance a viable business. If Henry Tyrer had attempted to establish himself with such a small sum it would have meant a 'hand to mouth' existence with little chance of building up the capital which was essential if he was to take advantage of whatever opportunities came his way. Tyrer's own resources at this time were obviously very small and he felt that he could not call upon his family for financial support. The banks of the day were also extremely reluctant to advance sums to those like Tyrer who were both young and without collateral and, recognising this fact, perhaps, there is no record of any attempt to obtain overdraft facilities until very much later.[10]

Henry Tyrer attached much importance to his independence and so was anxious to avoid taking a partner. He therefore entered into business on his own account quite free of any attachments but soon discovered that lack of capital was an even greater constraint than he had anticipated. This forced him to reconsider earlier decisions and, after suitable negotiations, made an arrangement with Charles Hamilton of George J. Hamilton and Company, commission and forwarding agents, of Fenwick Street, Liverpool.[11] This undoubtedly constituted a partnership but never formally traded as such. Henry Tyrer and Company continued as before and as George J. Hamilton and Company did the same it appears that it was purely a financial arrangement whereby Hamilton provided working capital in return for a share in the profits. The amount of original investment is not known but in August 1885, Tyrer repaid a final sum of £400 and the 'partnership' was at an end.[12]

III

With the aid of the capital supplied by Charles Hamilton, Henry Tyrer was relieved of his most pressing financial problems and could concentrate on developing his business. Thus he was able to continue as a 'Commission Agent' as well as building up his interests in wines and spirits to such an extent that in 1883 he had to move his cooperage to more substantial premises in Greenland Street.[13] This generated further activity and by 1885 he was being described as a 'General Merchant'. Tyrer's work on a commission basis was, by then, obviously being supplemented, perhaps exceeded, by goods being exported and produce being imported on the firm's own account. This additional work required further office accommodation so the Company moved to Irwell Chambers in Fazakerly Street[14] — a site they were to occupy until 1888.[15]

In 1883 Heywood's Bank was taken over by the Bank of Liverpool. For some reason this led Henry Tyrer to transfer his account to another institution but by 1885 he wished to return to Heywood's as '. . . the Adelphi Bank is out of the way for him'.[16] As is customary on these occasions Tyrer gave his new manager a statement of his financial affairs and this showed the tremendous progress which his Company had made during its first five and a half years.

According to Tyrer's statement he had started his Company with £500 and he now controlled assets worth £2,300. The increase was entirely due to the earnings of his Company which was currently worth £2,000 – he also owned shares valued at £300 in the Congo and Central African Company Limited.[17] Tyrer stated that he only had one outstanding debt: 'He has to pay out in August £400 due to Hamilton, Charles, his late partner.'[18]

Thus at the beginning of 1885 Henry Tyrer's net position was that he had a capital of approximately £1,900 – a substantial increase over the £100 net with which he had entered business in 1879. He then estimated his turnover for the coming year at between £16,000 and £20,000 so not surprisingly Heywood's branch was happy to re-open his account. Almost at once, however, came a minor dispute. This concerned the firm of Smallwood and Company who frequently purchased casks from Tyrers to send out to West Africa. On this occasion the bill which the Bank was asked to discount was for six instead of the normal three months and Tyrer had to explain that he had accepted the longer period as an inducement for Smallwood's to buy 150 instead of the 100 barrels originally ordered.[19]

Relations with the Bank Manager, Mr J.H. Shipley, remained harmonious in spite of this incident and Tyrer helped to maintain this situation by keeping the Bank fully informed of all developments. Thus in February, 1885, he reported a net profit 'after living' of £329 for the half-year beginning in June 1884. His living expenses were apparently very light, mainly because he continued to live with his parents at Ormskirk and were '. . . less than £100 a half-year after paying £25 life assurance premium'.[20] Tyrer also mentioned that he had discharged his old foreman and had replaced him with an excellent employee who was now in complete charge of the cooperage. Tyrer further informed the Bank that he was giving up part of his 'Commission' work so that he could devote more time to the cooperage as that side of the business was particularly busy and profitable.[21]

By 1885, when Henry Tyrer was in his twenty-seventh year, he could certainly claim to have established a solid business which was capable of providing him with a comfortable and reliable income. Tyrer's achievements in Liverpool then enabled him to think of marriage

and he turned his thoughts toward Jane Elizabeth Porter, a local young
lady of good family. Subsequent events show that this was to be a
long-lasting and romantic attachment so it may be presumed that the
young lady in question fully reciprocated his affection. However, in
the social climate of the times, it is doubtful if her parents would have
permitted, let alone welcomed, his attentions if he had not already
demonstrated his true potential in the conduct of his affairs.

IV

The tiny village of Rufford lies five miles to the north east of Ormskirk
and, like Burscough, was and remains almost totally devoted to agriculture. In the second half of the nineteenth century the sole landowner was Sir Thomas George Fermor-Hesketh and he was a man who
was deeply interested in enhancing the productivity of his soil. A large
part of his holdings were inundated during the winter months by the
waters of the adjoining Martin Mere but in 1849 he purchased a steam
engine and had it erected at Holmeswood. This could move approximately 28 tons of water per minute and with its aid a substantial
additional acreage was brought into cultivation.[22]

Hesketh's preoccupation with agriculture meant that his land agent
had a more than usually demanding occupation. Apart from being
responsible for the 400 acres of the family seat at Rufford (New) Hall
he would also have to oversee the whole of the tenanted land which
amounted to nearly three thousand acres within the parish together
with additional amounts outside its boundaries. David Boosnae[23] was
the occupier of this onerous position when the work of reclamation
began but when he decided to leave he was replaced by John Porter.

The Porter family had farmed in the Rufford area for many years[24]
but John Porter was destined for a different, though closely allied,
career. He was born in the parish in 1820 and after a simple education
at the local school joined the Hesketh estate offices as a junior clerk. He
was then only twelve years of age but proved to be so bright and
industrious that by the time he was twenty he had been promoted to
head clerk and in 1853 was appointed to be agent for all of Hesketh's
Lancashire estates.[25]

During John's stewardship the marsh at Hesketh Bank was reclaimed
and the enclosed area subsequently proved to be 'one of the most
fertile spots in Great Britain'.[26] Recognition of his valuable service was
marked by the presentation of numerous gifts and by the achievement
of a very substantial salary.[27] This enabled him to live in some style at
Beech House in Rufford, where he employed at least three servants,[28]

and his two children, Thomas Charles and Jane Elizabeth, were brought up with every comfort.

John Porter retired in 1878 at the age of 58 after 46 years in Hesketh's service. He then settled down to the life of a country gentleman continuing, of course, to take a full part in the activities of the district. Thus he was the founder of the Rufford Agricultural Society, a member of the Leyland Hundred Highway Board, a trustee for Peter Lathom's Charity and Treasurer of the Penny Savings Bank. He also took an active part in religious affairs and was people's warden at Rufford Parish Church for no less than twenty-four years.[29]

Jane Elizabeth Porter was born in 1855 and as she grew up is said to have been a vivacious and petite young lady who 'played a useful part in the village life, teaching in the Sunday School at St Mary's and acting as organist at the church on Sundays'.[30] It is not known when she and Henry Tyrer first met but the nearness of their homes and the relative sparseness of the local population would have made acquaintanceship almost inevitable. Tyrer's work in Liverpool would not have interrupted any friendship between the two as he continued to live at home and, as his career progressed, he would inevitably have been considered a more suitable prospect for matrimony.

In a small and fairly static, rural, community the choice of marriage partners would be strictly limited and Jane Elizabeth remained single until she was thirty. It is tempting to postulate that she waited for Henry Tyrer until he could prove to her father that he was worthy of her, but it might equally well be suggested that during an era when women of twenty-five were regarded as confirmed spinsters, both she and her family would have been pleased to have received a proposal at a much earlier stage.

Whatever is the truth of this surmise, Henry Tyrer and Jane Porter were married at Rufford Church on 17 June 1885, and this was to mark the beginning of a happy and prosperous partnership that lasted for over fifty-one years. Their first home was at 43 Greenbank Road, in the Tranmere district of Birkenhead.[31] It must have been extremely simple for Tyrer to travel to his office in the Liverpool centre from this address for there were frequent tram and ferry services. Consequently, during a period when he worked both early and late, Tranmere proved to be a very convenient base, but it was while living there that Henry and Jane suffered their worst disappointments. In May 1886, their first child – a girl – died after only eight days and two years later their second child – a boy – died at the age of seven months.[32]

These setbacks served to bring the Tyrers ever closer together and they appear to have spent much of their leisure in quiet, domestic pursuits. In particular they developed a major interest in gardening and this, together with the attractions of the countryside, decided them to seek a change and, in 1894,[33] they moved to Pygon's Hill House in Lydiate. Their new residence was a substantial old house about three miles south west of Ormskirk and was thus situated very near to the homes of their respective families and friends. Lydiate also enjoyed easy access to Liverpool by train and the Tyrer's found that their home was so comfortable and pleasant that they were to stay there for nearly twelve years. During this time they took an active interest in the affairs of the village and also continued to spend a great deal of energy in the growing of fruit, flowers and vegetables. It seems, in fact, that it was the challenge of a new and larger estate that finally persuaded them to move again and, in 1906, soon after the death of Jane's father,[34] they purchased 'Bewcastle' at Lathom.[35]

This was to be the Tyrer's final move and during the following thirty years they converted it into one of the 'show places' of south west Lancashire. The garden was considered to be especially beautiful with a number of rose arbours and walks, a rock garden and a very fine ornamental pool. The cultivation of roses became Henry's favourite hobby and '. . . his lovely gardens at "Bewcastle" in summer, bear eloquent testimony to the genius and care which he has devoted to the growing of the Queen of Flowers'.[36]

V

Tyrer's marriage and the consequent changes in his domestic arrangements did not alter his determination to further develop his business interests. His new responsibilities may, in fact, have stimulated even greater efforts and he continued to make good progress. This was made very clear during an interview with his Bank Manager which took place about ten months after his wedding: 'Mr Henry Tyrer tells Mr Shipley he is doing very well. He added £500 to his capital last year and it now stands at £2,500. His stock is easily realisable and his book debts are good.'[37]

A more comprehensive statement showing the position of Henry Tyrer and Company on 31 December 1886, indicates that the firm was growing rapidly and making even greater profits (see below).[38]

The difference between the liabilities and assets amounts to £3,940 and even if an allowance of £216 is made for possible bad debts the net figure remains a healthy £3,272. The Bank Manager thought that Tyrer's ship, the *Kawshawgha*,[39] was worth at least £750 so the true

Assets		Liabilities	
Value of property	£440	Corporation of Liverpool	
80 shares in the		(for land)	£320
Congo Co	240	Bills payable	940
Ship	500	Open account	1,486
Stock	2,600		
Book debts	1,600		
Cash and Bills in			
hand	856		
Total:	£6,236		£2,746

position was better than is demonstrated above and Mr Shipley came to the conclusion that Henry Tyrer personally was 'worth a good £3,500 because he has £300 to £400 of furniture'.[40]

Tyrer's position, however, was not quite as favourable as was thought because of what proved to be a disastrous investment in the Congo and Central African Company Limited. This firm had been formed in March 1882, to '. . . take over as a going concern and work the business of an African Merchant, for some years past carried on by Isaac Zagury, at certain factories and agencies on or near the River Congo and the neighbouring settlements'.[41]

When it was established the Company opened an office in London but it was quickly appreciated that premises in Liverpool would produce better results and the head office was moved to 62 Dale Street, at the end of July 1882. At that time the business had an issued capital of only £10,092 but this gradually increased and by 1885 had risen to £42,038.[42] One of the original subscribers was William Griffith Leete, a broker of 7 Rumford Street, whose office was only a few yards away from that of Henry Tyrer. It seems likely, therefore, that it was Mr Leete who persuaded Tyrer to invest in the firm, perhaps on the understanding that the Company's cooperage would then receive preferential treatment when barrels and casks were required!

The only certainty is that Tyrer purchased 100 shares at £5 in 1883 and that he sold twenty of them the following year. This left him with an investment of £400 (80 x £5) when, in 1886, an Extra-Ordinary General Meeting agreed that the Congo Company be voluntarily liquidated. The winding-up process began at once but was not completed until 1895 when it was reported that the 'Land and buildings in Africa are now absolutely worthless'.[43] Tyrer still owned 80 shares but as only 2s 6d per share could be recovered he received the sum of £10 and thus suffered a net loss of £390.[44]

In itself this loss was not a vital blow but it did come at an awkward time when Tyrer's were continuing to grow at a rapid rate and needed all the capital they could obtain. This can be seen by the acquisition of an even larger cooperage at 91 Jordon Street in 1887[45] and by its expansion to include 89 Jordon Street in 1888.[46] The resulting trade, however, does not seem to have justified this investment and a first hint of trouble is noted in November 1888, when the Bank noted that Tyrer was £400 overdrawn 'without any definite understanding'.[47] This does not appear to have been a major difficulty for Tyrer explained that he was heavily stocked with casks and did not expect to move many until the following January. Tyrer also seems to have been able to reassure the Bank by proposing to sell the *Kawshawgha* for £1,500 (three times what he paid for her) and there the matter was allowed to rest.

Unfortunately trade did not improve in 1889, although Tyrer's commitments had risen, and in spite of all his efforts he gradually fell into an ill-liquid position. Consequently he was forced, on the 12 June 1890, to call a meeting of his creditors and his accounts then showed liabilities of £14,000 and assets of barely £9,000.[48] This situation was really one of insolvency but Tyrer was not made bankrupt. The creditors clearly took the view that it would be better to let him continue to trade and hope that he could overcome his problems rather than accept a certain loss of at least £5,000.

Henry Tyrer's ability to make an arrangement with his creditors demonstrates that the business community in Liverpool still regarded him with some degree of confidence. To retain that respect Tyrer worked harder than ever and ensured that he realised his assets at the best possible prices. His main physical asset was, of course, his cooperage and the sale of this to Mr Michael Mannion[49] in December 1890, did much to satisfy his most pressing needs. Tyrer's business then consisted of shipping and forwarding, the operation of buying agencies for various London merchants engaged in the West African trade and a continuing interest in Lager and Beer.[50] Tyrer also indicated to his new bank manager, Mr C.A. Stephens, that he was being increasingly employed as a shipping agent by James Knott of the Prince Line and that he expected that he would soon have to devote all his time to this new entrant on to the West African shipping routes.[51]

Tyrer's relationship with the Prince Line did, indeed, occupy a great deal of his time but did not develop in the way that he had anticipated.[52] Accordingly, in July 1891, he executed a Deed of Assignment which transferred the agency to Messrs Japp and Kirby. This, it was stated, was done for the benefit of his creditors[53] but whether this refers to the original debts accumulated by Henry Tyrer and Company, or to new losses[54] incurred with the Prince Line cannot now be determined.

Tyrer then attempted to persuade his bank to end all the restrictions that had been imposed in June 1890, but the manager would not permit this until all of his creditors had agreed. The sale of the cooperage and of the Prince Line agency together with other realisations and accumulated profits subsequently enabled him to settle all outstanding claims, however, and the bank then lifted all of its remaining constraints.

The principal difficulty then facing Henry Tyrer was the lack of working capital. This was overcome to a limited extent by the granting of overdraft facilities against the security of deeds in respect of a property in Town Green deposited by Mrs Tyrer.[55] As Henry's business slowly picked up he was again handicapped by a shortage of capital so in December 1893, his wife came to the rescue once more by depositing further deeds.[56] Clearly Tyrer owed much to his wife for her support in these difficult times and it seems probable that it was the knowledge of her financial status that assisted him to stave off his creditors when bankruptcy appeared an almost inevitable fate. Mrs Tyrer's faith in her husband was quickly justified, however, for he made steady progress, in spite of many abortive attempts to enter the West African shipping trade,[57] and his Company went from strength to strength. So much so that only twelve years after escaping virtual bankruptcy he had a capital of £7,000 and was seeking advice from the bank in respect of a £2,500 investment in real estate.[58]

It is a long-standing tradition within his Company that Henry Tyrer went bankrupt during his early years in business.[59] This is undoubtedly a reference to the events of 1890 when he certainly experienced great difficulties but was never declared to be insolvent in a legal sense. According to *The Times* only three people with the surname of Tyrer went bankrupt during the period from 1889 to 1892.[60] These included James Tyrer, an oil and colour dealer of Walsall[61] and William Walker Tyrer, a hotel keeper of Ryde, Isle of Wight,[62] who obviously had nothing to do with the Tyrers of the Ormskirk district. The third was a John Tyrer of Skelmersdale, near Ormskirk, and as both Henry's father and one of his brothers bore that name he appears to be worthy of further investigation.

This John Tyrer, described as a 'draper and tea dealer, formerly greengrocer, more recently tea and smallware dealer' had a receiving order made against him in June 1890,[63] and appeared before the

Official Receiver in July of that year. In his evidence Tyrer stated that he was originally a collier who had gone into business as a draper and tea merchant with very little capital and that it was this, together with bad trade that had caused his downfall. Significantly, however, there is no suggestion that he was engaged in farming at any time.[64]

By 1890 Henry's father, John Tyrer senior, had retired from a life-time of farming so cannot possibly be confused with his namesake. His son, John Tyrer junior — Henry's brother — also spent his whole life engaged in agriculture and his obituary[65] lists the many important offices he held including Chairman of the Farm Committee of the Board of Guardians and an active member of the Lancashire Farmers Association. He, too, bears no resemblance to the John Tyrer, 'draper and tea dealer' who was examined at Liverpool Bankruptcy Court. It is quite certain, therefore, that this John Tyrer had no connection with Henry Tyrer or his family and that it was just a coincidence that he should be declared bankrupt at about the same time that Henry Tyrer and Company were experiencing difficulties of their own.

Notes

1. *Arthur Heywood, Sons & Company, 1773-1883*, a short history published by Martins Bank Ltd, Water Street, Liverpool, 1967.

2. Heywood's Bank is now Heywood's Branch of Barclays Bank. It still occupies the same building as it did when Henry Tyrer opened his account. References to its archives are given as Heywood's MSS, Customers' Working Accounts, vol. 1, 14 July 1879.

3. Ibid.

4. Ibid.

5. Gores' *Liverpool Directory*, 1880.

6. Ibid., 1882.

7. There is no mention of James Murdoch in Gores' *Liverpool Directory* after 1882. Due to the twelve month lag in publication this probably means that he retired and left the area in 1881.

8. *Shipping*, 'Shipping Sidelights', 1 April 1895, p. 534.

9. John Tyrer died in 1894 and after small legacies his estate was divided amongst his seven surviving children in equal parts. Probate was granted at Liverpool on 18 January 1895, and his effects were then valued at £532 8s 6d.

10. Heywood's MSS. The Annual Diaries indicate that although they discounted bills for Tyrer after 1885 it was not until 1888 that he asked for an overdraft.

11. Gores' *Liverpool Directory*, 1880.

12. Heywood's MSS, Annual Diary, 2 January 1885.

13. Gores' *Liverpool Directory*, 1883.

14. Ibid., 1885.

15. Ibid., 1888.

16. Heywood's MSS, Annual Diary, 1 January 1885.

17. Ibid.

18. Ibid., 2 January 1885.
19. Ibid., 3 January 1885.
20. Ibid., 18 February 1885. The high level of insurance carried by Henry Tyrer may have been part of the arrangement which he had made with his former partner.
21. Ibid.
22. Kelly's *Lancashire Directory*, 1854, p. 173.
23. Ibid., p. 175.
24. The local directories show that Henry Porter was listed as a farmer in 1854 and Henry George Porter was shown as a farmer in 1887.
25. *Ormskirk Advertiser*, Obituary of John Porter, 27 July 1905.
26. Ibid.
27. When Porter died in 1905 his effects were valued at £15,273 13s 10d (probate was granted at Lancaster on 15 August 1905).
28. Ibid.
29. Ibid.
30. *Ormskirk Advertiser*, 'A Lathom Golden Wedding', 20 June 1935.
31. Gores' *Liverpool Directory*, 1886.
32. These were Louise Frances, born 7 May and died 15 May 1886, and Harry Cuthbert, born 18 March and died 15 October 1888. They were buried at Rufford Church and both of their parents now lie in the same grave.
33. Gores' *Liverpool Directory*, 1894.
34. The timing of the move may well have been influenced by the death of John Porter for Jane Tyrer benefited substantially from his estate.
35. Lathom is situated two to three miles to the north east of Ormskirk.
36. *Ormskirk Advertiser*, 'A Lathom Golden Wedding', 20 June 1935.
37. Heywood's MSS, Annual Diary, 29 April 1886.
38. Ibid., 19 February 1887.
39. This is the first mention of Tyrer owning a ship and it appears to have been purchased fairly recently. It is likely that it was a very small vessel which Tyrer used in the coastal trades.
40. Heywood's MSS, Annual Diary, 19 February 1887.
41. The remaining records of the Congo and Central African Co Ltd, Registration Number: 16547 are to be found at the Public Record Office, Kew (References BT34: Box 294 and BT31: Box 2954).
42. Henry Tyrer MSS, Box 8, Extracts from files at the Public Record Office.
43. Ibid.
44. Ibid.
45. Gores' *Liverpool Directory*, 1888.
46. Ibid., 1889.
47. Heywood's MSS, Annual Diary, 15 November 1888.
48. Ibid., 12 June 1890.
49. Gores' *Liverpool Directory*, 1890, describes him as a 'Cooper and Hoop Merchant', with works in Regent Road, Walter Street and Vauxhall Road, Liverpool.
50. Heywood's MSS, Annual Diary, 6 December 1890.
51. Ibid.
52. See below, Chapter 3, pp. 39-41.
53. Heywood's MSS, Annual Diary, 22 September 1891.
54. See below, Chapter 3, p. 40.
55. Heywood's MSS, Annual Diary, 13 August 1892.
56. Ibid., 7 December 1893.
57. See below, Chapter 3, pp. 41-3.
58. Heywood's MSS, Manager's Minute Book, 2A, 10 November 1903, p. 277.

59. Author's interviews with Mr F. Cutts during the early 1960s.

60. Samuel Palmer, *Index to The Times*, Richmond House, Shepperton-on-Thames.

61. *The Times*, 23 March 1889, p. 13e.

62. Ibid., 3 January 1890, p. 7d.

63. Ibid., 25 June 1890, p. 12b.

64. *Ormskirk Advertiser*, 17 July 1890 and 31 July 1890.

65. Ibid., Obituary of John Tyrer, 17 August 1911.

3 HENRY TYRER AND THE WEST AFRICAN SHIPPING TRADE

I

The last English slave ship, the *Kitty's Amelia*, left the Mersey on 27 July 1807.[1] This brought to an end Liverpool's connection with the transatlantic slave trade and considerably reduced the number of its ships that sailed to West Africa.[2] Gradually, however, the export of traditional commodities — which had never ended in the slave era — began to increase in response to the industrialisation of the United Kingdom. This was particularly marked in respect of palm oil and while only 55 tons had been imported into Liverpool in 1785 the amount had risen to 1,000 tons by 1810 and to 30,000 tons in 1851.[3] These were extremely high quantities and the system of shipment whereby each firm of merchants owned its own sailing vessels became more and more inadequate. Pressure thus developed for the establishment of regular steam shipping services and, in 1852, this opportunity was seized by MacGregor Laird.[4]

Laird had been born in 1809 and was a member of the Birkenhead family of shipbuilders.[5] He was educated at Edinburgh and, after a brief interlude with the family firm, joined with Richard Lander to organise an expedition to explore the River Niger. This took place in 1832 but thirty-nine of the forty-eight members died of diseases and in these circumstances there seemed little point in making further efforts to develop trade links with the interior of West Africa.[6] Consequently Laird entered into a career with the shipping industry and, for a time, acted as Secretary for the British and North American Steam Navigation Company. Later, however, after a second spell with the family business, he moved to London and in 1849 established himself as an African Merchant.[7]

Laird was then in an excellent position to judge the growth of West African trade and undoubtedly noted that in 1850 the sailing vessels engaged on this route 'amounted to 40,410 tons outwards, and 42,057 inwards, and the quantity of tonnage actually carried may be fairly reckoned at one-third more'.[8] His personal experience on the Niger together with his understanding of the commercial possibilities of steam shipping then convinced Laird that a regular line would be a viable proposition. Accordingly he approached the Government and after

36

lengthy negotiations was able to obtain a mail contract which would provide a subsidy of over £21,000 per annum for a ten-year period. Armed with this contract Laird had no difficulty in attracting financial backing and, thus, was able to organise the African Steam Ship Company in 1852.[9]

The new line rapidly established regular sailings to West Africa and these radically changed the character of the trade as well as generating a substantial amount of additional business. Existing, large-scale, merchants found that they could manage with a smaller inventory for a given size of market as stocks could be replaced very quickly. They also found that they made considerable savings by having fewer goods in transit and so, in consequence, found it profitable and convenient to dispose of their own vessels. In addition, merchants with only limited resources found that they could now take part in the trade as it was no longer necessary for them to own or charter a complete ship. As a result many new firms began to operate on the Coast and the entire trade, '. . . acquired a fresh dynamism from their presence'.[10]

The sailings of the African Steam Ship Company were only moderately successful so long as London was its British base but when the terminal was moved to Liverpool in 1856 the line began to make reasonable profits. This was partly because Merseyside was the real centre of the trade but also because of the excellence of the firm's local agents. They were a small firm, originally organised by William and Hamilton Laird (brothers of MacGregor), but usually referred to as 'Fletcher and Parr' after their successors, who were highly efficient. This is not surprising for apart from its two partners it included Alexander Elder, John Dempster, John Holt and Alfred Jones amongst its staff — all men who were destined to make a significant contribution to the development of West African trade.[11]

When MacGregor Laird died in 1861 the African Steam Ship Company had achieved a position of dominance on West African shipping routes. Thereafter its directors chose to follow an extremely conservative policy which resulted in limited returns but minimum risks. The Company thus failed to expand, even though the demand for its services was rising, and in 1868 it paid the price when a new firm entered the trade. This was the British and African Steam Navigation Company Limited, and it was all the more unwelcome because it had been promoted by two of its own ex-employees, John Dempster and Alexander Elder.[12]

A period of severe competition followed but by 1870 an arrangement had been made whereby the African Steam Ship Company agreed to co-operate with the British and African Steam Navigation Company. This was put into operation by the respective agents of the two firms — Fletcher and Parr and Elder Dempster and Company. An internal disagreement within the African Steam Ship Company then led to Fletcher and Parr losing its agency and the Company opened its own branch office in Liverpool. This meant that there was less scope for Alfred Jones within Messrs Fletcher and Parr's business so he decided to leave and establish his own firm.[13]

II

Alfred Lewis Jones, who was later to prove a major obstacle to Henry Tyrer's attempts to enter the West African shipping trade, had been born in Carmarthen in 1845. His family moved to Liverpool when he was a small child so when the time came for him to look for a career the sea appeared as an obvious choice. Jones did make one voyage as a cabin boy with the African Steam Ship Company but then, in 1860, he joined Messrs Fletcher and Parr as a junior clerk.[14] He stayed with this firm during its struggle with the British and African and played some part in promoting the subsequent agreement between the two lines. The loss of the African agency in 1875 then led Jones to re-appraise his prospects with Fletcher and Parr and, in 1878, set up in business on his own account, trading as Alfred L. Jones and Company. This development alarmed Elder and Dempster for, as former colleagues, they recognised his true potential. Accordingly they decided to offer him a junior partnership in their firm and, after careful consideration, Jones joined them in October, 1879.[15]

Within five years Jones had become a senior partner of Elder Dempster and Company and then completely controlled the firm until his death in 1909.[16] Elder Dempster, in 1884, was a relatively small shipping agency whose only real asset was a precarious hold on the two British lines which operated on West African routes. At this time the activities of interlopers and rival lines provided Jones with many problems. Fortunately for him difficulties of this kind helped to cement the relationship between the African Steam Ship Company and the British and African Steam Navigation Company and with a united front he was able to maintain what subsequently became a monopoly of the carrying trade to the West African coast.

Jones understood that the co-operation between the two British lines was an essential pre-requisite to his strength so he gradually secured a financial interest in both so that he was able to influence and, eventually, to lay down their policies.[17] Jones also appreciated that control of the 'surf boats' on the almost harbourless seaboard of West Africa had a special significance and took steps to secure them for the exclusive use of his shippers.[18] By 1890, therefore, Jones enjoyed a very strong position. A few merchants still retained a number of small sailing vessels and the Woermann Line of Hamburg provided limited services from the Continent to both the German and British colonies on the Coast. With these exceptions Elder Dempster, under Jones, were responsible for the carriage of just about all cargoes both into and out of West Africa. This meant that both the African and the British and African lines obtained sound financial results and, in turn, led to Alfred Jones improving his power and his fortune.[19]

III

Henry Tyrer's working life began in 1872 when he became an assistant to James Murdoch who specialised as a merchant dealing with West Africa. During the ensuing seven years Tyrer learned an enormous amount about the pecularities and possibilities of this particular trade so when he started on his own account his business retained a strong West African flavour. Tyrer's interests were, of course, as a commission and general merchant and as a buying agent. He also diversified into cooperage as this was a necessary part of both his palm oil and liquor trades. Until 1890, however, Tyrer's interest in shipping was confined to the *Kawshawgha* which only operated in coastal waters[20] but as a substantial shipper to and from West Africa he must have been aware of Alfred Jones' activities and of his financial success.

Sometime in 1890, during a period when his business affairs were causing him some anxiety, Tyrer seems to have decided that the West African shipping trade offered such lucrative returns that he could no longer leave it in the sole hands of Alfred Jones. By then an average of over 50,000 tons of palm oil per year was being imported from the Coast[21] and many other commodities were increasing in volume and value.[22] Tyrer's special knowledge of the trade then enabled him to convince James Knott of the Prince Line that a profitable opportunity existed and Tyrer was appointed as his Liverpool agent.[23]

Once committed, James Knott entered enthusiastically into the West African trade and refused to be put off by Alfred Jones.[24] He then sought and received encouragement from John Holt and boasted that he would build between 'twelve and twenty vessels' of advanced design specially for this route if Holt and some of the other merchants would support him.[25] Knott then ordered a number of these ships[26] although he was already experiencing difficulty in obtaining cargo for the tonnage he had placed in this service. Knott wondered, therefore, if Tyrer was the best man to act as his agent '. . . he has worked hard and done his best but is inexperienced (in shipping) and lacks position with the shippers — he has not taken a dignified stand.'[27]

As an example of Tyrer's inexperience in these matters Knott went on to write —

> . . . It has occurred to me the last day or two that the shipping and chartering (for the Government) may be in the hands of an upper clerk or official and if so then that might account for a great deal, if I am right then this gentleman must be too cute for Mr T. and may be actuated with more zeal than scruple . . .[28]

Whatever reservations Knott had about Tyrer were confirmed in June 1891, and he found it necessary to send a long telegram to Holt who he regarded as his major ally in Liverpool —

> Tyrer writes informing me he is in financial difficulties and owing Prince Steamers over 1600 pounds. I will have to appoint new agent and take steps to protect myself but dont want to do anything so that this may leak out. I think it might be handled in discreet manner so that we dont give ourselves away to many and otherwise injure ourselves. My idea would be to hand agency over to someone else. Not to say why it has been done and let Tyrer go to whoever is appointed and be with them for a few weeks until everything is straightened up and put in order and he could make what excuse he liked.[29]

James Knott then looked for another agent to represent him in Liverpool and with some difficulty, avidly fermented by Alfred Jones, appointed Messrs Japp and Kirby.[30] They, however, had no more success than Henry Tyrer and in 1892 the Prince Line withdrew from West African routes. In a letter to Holt, explaining why he was withdrawing from the trade, Knott made it clear that it was the lack of bulk cargoes for the outward run (which only the Crown Agents could supply) and the failure of the merchants to give him real support that were at the root of his problems. He also described some of the impediments which Jones was able to put in his way in West Africa —

> . . . while writing you I would wish to name the detention suffered at the (Oil) Rivers, and the Rivers only, part of this is explained by

the African Association's Agents systematically giving the preference to what they call the Mail Boats, even when our ships had been there some time, immediately the others arrived work was either stopped on ours altogether or practically and all the energy and interest centred on the others to get them away . . . consequently our ships with their present appliances on board could easily discharge and load in twelve days, . . . why should they be there regularly six and eight weeks . . . ?[31]

IV

Henry Tyrer's loss of the Prince Line agency was a severe setback for him but, as noted above,[32] with the aid of his wife he gradually regained full solvency and his company once again made good progress. Tyrer's business continued to be devoted mainly to agency work of all descriptions and this included a substantial amount as a shipping agent.[33] Some, though not all, of this was concerned with West Africa so Tyrer was kept closely in touch with the shipping services to that region and was well aware of the further advances being made by Alfred Jones. He, therefore, made every effort to encourage other lines to enter the trade and, in 1894, was appointed as Liverpool agent to the London based General Steam Navigation Company.

The sailings of the new operator became the subject of much controversy in the *Journal of Commerce*, as a letter from an 'Old African' denied the need for the competition.[34] Henry Tyrer claimed the opposite[35] and followed this up with a second letter to the Editor in which he gave details of a new record established by the *Cygnet* which had delivered freight to Lagos in only twenty-seven days.[36] Unfortunately sufficient merchants were not attracted to use the new facility and an extension of the service up the freshly opened Manchester Ship Canal did little to create sufficient cargoes.[37] Consequently when the General Steam Navigation Company published its trading figures for 1894 it was seen that the firm had made a substantial loss and no dividend could be paid.[38] The Company's Report was full of the problems caused by Elder Dempster and a 'Disgusted Shareholder' wrote to the press complaining that it should never have attempted to enter into competition with such a strong shipping line.[39]

Once again Alfred Jones had used his influence with both government departments and the merchants' associations to prevent a new line from becoming established. In addition he cut freight rates to the bone on the appropriate services and used his control of the 'boating companies' and of the Bank of British West Africa[40] to make it almost impossible for anyone to gain a footing in the trade. All of Tyrer's pleadings could not disguise these unpleasant facts and in June 1895, the General Steam Navigation Company withdrew its services to West Africa.[41]

Tyrer was not, of course, happy with this turn of events and remained convinced that a properly organised line would make tremendous profits if it could gain the support of the merchant community. When, almost at once, he approached and gained the interest of Sir Christopher Furness of Messrs Furness Withy, a shipbuilding firm, he got in touch with John Holt —

> The idea is to form a Company — say the Liverpool and African Steamship Shippers Company — with sufficient capital to build five steamers and a branch boat for Lagos, issuing a prospectus and getting as much as possible subscribed by the general body of Shippers, and his firm would take a large interest in it and find suitable steamers to run the trade while the new steamers were being built, and Sir Christopher would consent to be chairman and would undertake to secure an influential Board of Directors, but thinks two or three leading shippers ought also to be on the Board. Would you be willing to meet Sir Christopher . . . ?[42]

At first John Holt welcomed the proposed new line and urged George Miller[43] to give it his support.[44] It was then proposed that the new firm should be called the West African Traders Company Limited, and Holt was so impressed that he wrote to Miller —

> The more I think of the proposal made us the more convinced I am that if we miss this opportunity we shall never have another, and that we shall heartily deserve anything that follows the missing of so promising a chance . . .[45]

John Holt succeeded in interesting Miller to some extent and a meeting to include Furness, Tyrer, Miller and Holt was arranged for the end of October 1895. Before this took place, however, Furness wrote to Holt giving details of the financial stake that he expected the merchants to take in the new shipping line. This had the effect of convincing Holt that the proposed firm was not a practical idea and he refused to attend the meeting. Instead he wrote to Furness as follows —

> I have delayed replying to your kind letter of 10th Inst. with a view

to seeing whether there was any likelihood of Messrs Millers and ourselves subscribing £100,000 for ordinary shares. I do not see that this has been advanced since I last saw you. My firm is not disposed to take half, nor do I see that Messrs Millers are disposed to take half the £100,000. The (African) Association I do not expect to be able to influence in the direction of taking an interest at the outset. I feel that you have offered in the way of finance all that could be expected of you, and if the shippers as a whole have not responded, you have no encouragement whatever to go on with the scheme. I would not advise you to do anything without a guarantee in some binding form, from the principal shippers to give you a minimum rate of freight.[46]

Henry Tyrer did all he could to persuade Holt to come to the meeting in London but he refused. Subsequent letters from Furness Withy suggested that if Holt and Miller would subscribe £25,000 each, the shipbuilders would find the balance. Holt wrote to Miller but when he received no reply came to the conclusion that Miller was not prepared to take part. When this was confirmed by Tyrer, Holt wrote to Furness withdrawing completely and the proposal came to an end.[47]

V

Henry Tyrer's attempts to enter the West African shipping trade had been singularly unsuccessful and in spite of all his efforts he had been able to make little progress. The failure of the negotiations with Furness Withy demonstrated the basic problem. The merchants were anxious to co-operate to reduce the cost of shipping to and from West Africa but were not prepared to follow this policy to its logical conclusion and end their competition on the Coast.[48] Consequently they viewed one another's activities with the deepest suspicion and each was determined that no one should gain a competitive advantage. In these circumstances co-operation was impossible and schemes for the co-ownership of shipping facilities were not practical.

It seems that by 1895 Henry Tyrer had accepted that he was unlikely to be able to break into West African shipping but any remaining doubts were finally dispelled when Alfred Jones organised a shipping conference to regulate the trade. The ending of the sailings of the General Steam Navigation Company in June 1895, had solved an immediate problem but Jones was sure that other rival lines would soon appear. He was particularly concerned that either the Royal Niger Company or the African Association, or both, might make their own arrangements for their goods to be shipped for they controlled substantial cargoes. He was also aware of Tyrer's negotiations with Sir Christopher Furness and feared that at some stage they might succeed or be resurrected in some other form. He therefore consulted his only real competitor, the Woermann Line of Hamburg and, with its approval, began the first moves that would ensure him a more permanent control of West African shipping routes.

The first deep-sea shipping conference had been created in the Calcutta trade in 1877 and, by 1895, they included most of the world's important shipping routes.[49] With many such precedents it is not surprising that Alfred Jones chose to impose a similar institution on the West African trade, in fact the only mystery is why he had not done so at an earlier date. George Miller described the new system when giving evidence to the Royal Commission on Shipping Rings,[50] saying that the first he knew of it was when a letter came through the post. This announced that all freights were to be increased by 10% and that this addition was to be known as 'primage'.[51] It also stated that all merchants must sign a declaration that all their shipments for the next six months would be made by the conference lines i.e., the African Steam Ship Company, the British and African Steam Navigation Company or the Woermann Line. It then went on to inform the shippers that after six months exclusive shipment with the conference that the 'primage' could be claimed back as a rebate, but that this would not be paid until after a further period of six months exclusive carriage by the conference.[52]

Miller and the other merchants had only a month in which to decide to join the conference and in the absence of a suitable alternative he chose to sign the declaration. He could have provided his own ships or joined with others to make different arrangements but this would have been expensive and time-consuming. Miller's example was followed by the remainder of the merchants and once having shipped under the new conditions the deferred rebate system ensured their continual loyalty. To a merchant like John Holt a sum of £10,000 would always be owing to him for although it was being regularly repaid it was simultaneously being replaced by fresh payments of primage. This was a virtually irresistible argument for him to continue to use the conference services and it affected the big and small alike in direct proportion to their shipments. Consequently, the introduction of the system on to West African routes meant that few attempts were subsequently made to enter the trade and with its aid the tiny, but growing, fleet of the African Association was removed from contention in 1896.[53]

VI

The West African Shipping Conference was only challenged three times in the period from 1895 to the death of Jones at the end of 1909. One attempt to put ships on the route was made by the Gold Coast Mining Companies who established the Sun Line using chartered tonnage in 1906. Unfortunately for its owners this was not a success as the deferred rebate system was too strong to allow the service to attract any return cargoes[54] and it went out of business in 1908. A second challenge made to the conference was by the Hamburg-Bremen Africa Line which, in 1907, started a service in direct opposition to the Woermann Line. The eventual outcome was a financial arrangement with Woermann and can best be regarded as a re-organisation of the German side of the conference structure.[55] The other and final attempt to oppose Jones' control of the trade was made by Henry Tyrer.

Following the collapse of his efforts to persuade Sir Christopher Furness to establish a new line and taking into account the power of the newly formed conference structure Henry Tyrer had abandoned his attempts to interest shipowners and merchants in an independent company that would provide services to West Africa. He busied himself with other aspects of his growing firm and while he retained much concern for African trade the diversification of his business meant that he was no longer actively involved on a day-to-day basis. Nevertheless, West Africa can never have been far from Tyrer's thoughts and, no doubt, the memory of his defeats still rankled. Consequently he was more than ready to take advantage of any favourable situations that might arise and, after a long wait, the first of several suitable opportunities presented itself in 1903.

By then Tyrer was involved in the importation of woodpulp from Scandinavia[56] and operated several small steamers between Preston and Scandinavia. At the beginning of 1903 a lull occurred in this trade and Tyrer decided to send *Prestonian* of 1,152 gross tons[57] out to West Africa. His decision was influenced by a meeting with Mr W.K. Findlay of W.B. MacIver and Company during which the difficulty of interesting the conference lines in logs had been discussed.[58] *Prestonian* took out a large general cargo of salt, stock fish and groceries and returned with large quantities of mahogany for MacIvers which she had loaded up river with her own gear. While out on the Coast the loading of the timber took longer than had been anticipated so after a long delay Henry Tyrer cabled to her captain: 'You must move heaven and earth to sail Saturday.' To which her master, Captain William Ker, replied: 'Heaven and earth immovable am raising hell.'[59] Nevertheless the voyage proved profitable so was repeated in 1904 but for a variety of reasons these sailings were not continued.

Alfred Jones was not pleased when he heard of the first voyage of *Prestonian* and arranged to see Mr Findlay at the earliest possible moment. During the interview which followed he threatened to withdraw the sum of £3,000 which he had invested in MacIvers and also pointed out that he was at liberty to retain the deferred rebate due from earlier shipments with the conference lines.[60] These threats were regarded as a warning by Findlay but in spite of them he thought he would support another voyage the following year as he was most anxious to move more of his timber.[61] He realised, however, that if he did not give a definite undertaking to Jones after the second voyage then the threats would be translated into action. It would, therefore, have been exceedingly difficult for Tyrer to have arranged a third voyage if he had needed MacIver's cargoes but, because of a personal aspect, the possibility did not arise.

On her second voyage *Prestonian* carried Henry Tyrer's nephew, John E. Wilson, as supercargo. He was provided with detailed instructions[62] in respect of every port of call and with regard to every commodity and it seems that he was being groomed to take a responsible position in the Company. All went well until the vessel reached Capstown, near Benin, and then a tragedy occurred –

No doubt you will have heard the dreadful news from Lagos which happened at Capstown, April 3rd at 5 pm. Mr Wilson, 2nd Mate and I went to bathe among the logs where all hands had been bathing all day. I did not get into the water at all, I was just washing myself, Mr Wilson and 2nd Mate were swimming when suddenly Mr Wilson threw up his hands and sunk very quickly, never shouted or made no sign and the Kroo boys and pilots – also Mr Neil's men dived down all over and could see nothing, the depth of water was 17 feet. 100 yards up the river, about one hour later a woman was drowned – its awful sad, I feel for you all as the news is so sad. I am glad for his Father and Mother and family's sake that on Tuesday 5th a native brought the body to Capstown, he saw an alligator trying to take the body to the bush. Well all honour was paid by everyone to the remains and (he was) buried about ¼ mile from Mr Neil's House – poor man . . .[63]

The shock of this disaster plus the other difficulties of the trade[64] so upset Henry Tyrer that he returned *Prestonian* to its usual route and it did not visit West Africa again. Apart from acting as Liverpool Agent for the ill-fated Sun Line Tyrer then took no further part in the West African shipping business until 1916 when the events of the First World War created an entirely different situation.[65]

Notes

1. Christopher Lloyd, *The Navy and the Slave Trade* (Longmans, London, 1939), p. 3.

2. D. Williams, 'Abolition and the Re-deployment of the Slave Fleet, 1807-11', *Journal of Transport History*, vol. 2, 1973, pp. 103-15, and B.K. Drake, 'Continuity and Flexibility in Liverpool's Trade with Africa and the Caribbean', *Business History*, vol. XVIII, no. 1, January 1976, pp. 85-97.

3. Allan McPhee, *The Economic Revolution in British West Africa* (George Routledge, London, 1926), p. 32.

4. P.N. Davies, *The Trade Makers: Elder Dempster in West Africa, 1852-1972* (George Allen and Unwin, London, 1973), pp. 35-41.

5. *Dictionary of National Biography*, 1892, vol. XXXI, p. 407. MacGregor Laird.

6. MacGregor Laird and R.A.K. Oldfield, *Narrative of an Expedition into the Interior of Africa by the River Niger . . .* (Richard Bentley, London, 1837), vol. 1.

7. Plumb and Howard, *West African Explorers* (Oxford University Press, London, 1955), pp. 465-83.

8. Statement (based on Parliamentary Returns) attached to the *Prospectus of the African Steam Ship Company* (ASP).

9. P.N. Davies, *The African Steam Ship Company, Liverpool and Merseyside*, J.R. Harris (ed.) (London, Frank Cass & Company, 1969).

10. P.N. Davies, 'The Impact of the Expatriate Shipping Lines on the Economic Development of British West Africa', *Business History*, vol. XIX, no. 1, January 1977, p. 9.

11. Davies, *The Trade Makers*, pp. 52-6.

12. Ibid., p. 51.

13. Ibid., pp. 59-66, 68-9.

14. P.N. Davies, 'Sir Alfred Jones and the Development of West African Trade', MA thesis, University of Liverpool, 1964, p. 20.

15. Ibid., p. 30.

16. Ibid., pp. 35-8 suggests reasons why Elder and Dempster 'retired' at 50 and 47 respectively.

17. Ibid., pp. 38-9.

18. Ibid., pp. 54-5.

19. Ibid., pp. 75-6.

20. See above, Chapter 2, p. 29.

21. It would have been a great deal more but the African producer was very sensitive to price movements and they fell consistently from 1855 to 1900. See McPhee, *The Economic Revolution in British West Africa*, footnote to p. 33.

22. Exports from British West Africa to the United Kingdom more than doubled in value from 1884 to 1900. See Appendix Table 2, p. 138.

23. Heywood's MSS, Annual Diary, 6 December 1890.

24. John Holt MSS, letter from James Knott to Henry Tyrer, 14 February 1891.

25. Ibid., letter from James Knott to John Holt, 19 March 1891.
26. Ibid., 24 March 1891.
27. Ibid., 12 May 1891.
28. Ibid.
29. Ibid., telegram from James Knott to John Holt, 9 June 1891.
30. Ibid., letter from James Knott to John Holt, 10 June 1891.
31. Ibid., letter from James Knott to John Holt (undated).
32. See above, Chapter 2, p. 32.
33. Heywood's MSS, Annual Diary, 7 December 1893.
34. *Journal of Commerce*, 10 February 1894.
35. Ibid., 27 February 1894.
36. Ibid., 21 March 1894.
37. Ibid., 10 October 1894.
38. *Financial News*, 19 February 1895.
39. *Journal of Commerce*, 26 February 1895.
40. R. Fry, *Bankers in West Africa (The Story of the Bank of British West Africa)* (Hutchinson Benham, London, 1976).
41. *Journal of Commerce*, 11 June 1895.
42. John Holt MSS, letter from Henry Tyrer to John Holt, 24 July 1895.
43. George Miller was the senior partner in Alexander Miller, Brother and Company. This was a Glasgow firm with interests in the Niger Basin, the Oil Rivers and the Gold Coast.
44. John Holt MSS, letter from John Holt to George Miller, 29 August 1895.
45. Ibid., 27 September 1895.
46. Ibid., letter from John Holt to Sir Christopher Furness, 17 October 1895.
47. Ibid., letter from John Holt to Furness Withy, 2 December 1895.
48. Ibid.
49. S. Marriner and F.E. Hyde, *The Senior, John Samuel Swire* (Liverpool University Press, 1967), pp. 61-73; and F.E. Hyde, *Shipping Enterprise and Management, Harrisons of Liverpool* (Liverpool University Press, 1967), pp. 69-74.
50. *Royal Commission on Shipping Rings* (HMSO), Cmnd 4668-70, 1909.
51. Primage was charged on all outward journeys and on palm oil and kernels on the homeward journey.
52. RCSR, evidence of George Miller, Q4311-14.
53. Davies, *The Trade Makers*, pp. 112-13.
54. RCSR, Appendices, Table 2, p. 196. Letter to the Colonial Office from John Rodger, Governor of the Gold Coast, 21 June 1907.
55. RCSR, evidence of J.H. Batty, Q6834.
56. See below Chapter 4, p. 54.
57. See below Chapter 4, p. 55.
58. Mr W.K. Findlay subsequently became Chairman of the Niger Company. The author of this present work was introduced to him by Mr Frederick Cutts of Henry Tyrer and Company in July 1965, when Mr Findlay was aged 97 and Mr Cutts was 84. See P.N. Davies, *Trading in West Africa* (ed.) (Croom Helm, London, 1976), pp. 137-8.
59. Author's interview with Mr F. Cutts, July 1965.
60. Author's interview with Mr Findlay, July 1965.
61. Logs were regarded as awkward cargo by the regular lines and, apart from a limited amount, always carried as deck cargo, they preferred to take other commodities if these were available.
62. Henry Tyrer MSS, Box 24, Instructions to Mr John E. Wilson, supercargo, s.s. *Prestonian*, 2nd voyage.
63. Ibid., letter from William Ker, Master of *Prestonian* to Henry Tyrer,

10 April 1904.
   64. Ibid.
   65. See below, Chapter 5, pp. 71-7.

GROWTH AND DIVERSIFICATION

Once Henry Tyrer had overcome the financial difficulties of the early 1890s he was anxious, once more, to expand his business. To this end he was prepared to investigate all opportunities as they presented themselves although not all worked out as he had anticipated. Thus by 1895 it was clear that he could not gain entry into the West African shipping trade[1] and a reference to him as a 'Manufacturing Perfumer' was not repeated and presumably was not a serious attempt at diversification.[2] The opening of the new dock at Preston in 1892 provided a more profitable outlet for Tyrer's enterprise[3] and complemented his activities at Liverpool where he continued to do well, both as a general merchant and in his capacity as a shipping, forwarding and commission agent. In 1893 Tyrer added shipbroking to his Liverpool operation[4] and soon afterwards was also being described as a 'loading broker'.[5]

By 1895, therefore, Henry Tyrer and Company were able to offer existing and potential clients a whole range of shipping and agency services. Tyrer subsequently built on these firm foundations by chartering coastal vessels and later entered into a number of cross-channel and short-sea trades by utilising both chartered and company owned tonnage.[6] The extension of these activities then led Tyrer to move from Rumford Place to Baltic Chambers in Red Cross Street where more commodious accommodation was available[7] and, for a brief period, he opened a second Liverpool office at 20 Chapel Street.[8] The latter was soon closed but branches of the firm were established at London[9] and at Salford, near Manchester,[10] while agencies were organised in Antwerp, Brussels and Rotterdam.

The consequences of this diversification was that by 1900 Tyrer had successfully widened the range and geographic spread of his business. The West African trade was no longer his main source of income although it was still important because, apart from the continuing agency work, the Company was still involved with a profitable aspect of the palm oil trade. Tyrer had, of course, sold his cooperage in 1890[11] but he retained his connection for American produced shooks[12] and supplied large quantities of these essential items to many firms of African merchants.

It would seem that Henry Tyrer had learned a great deal from his earlier mistakes and that, with a more mature judgement, had hit upon the correct formula for developing a viable business. He still retained his tremendous enthusiasm but tempered this with a moderate degree of caution. Consequently he built on the solid achievements of his Liverpool shipping and merchanting functions and his diversifications were really extensions of his existing business. By the turn of the century, therefore, Henry Tyrer and Company were well established in numerous profitable activities and Henry, himself, was beginning to reap the rewards of his enterprise. Thus by 1903 he estimated his capital at approximately £7,000[13] but by 1905 he was adding to this at the rate of about £2,000 per year after paying all expenses.[14]

II

The fact that Henry Tyrer had been brought up in the Ormskirk area meant that he was equally familiar with Liverpool and Preston for his home lay equidistant between the two ports. Tyrer chose to seek a career on the Mersey rather than the Ribble because the scale of operations were much larger and consequently offered greater opportunities. His success in establishing his business in Liverpool did not, however, prevent him from keeping an eye on progress at Preston and he took a particular interest in the widening and deepening of the channel to the sea. This work, begun in 1884, was to be completed by the excavation of a large new dock and Tyrer appreciated that this would lead to a vast expansion in the trade of the port and thus provide many fresh openings for his Company.

In the Spring of 1892, Tyrer obtained premises at 143 Church Street, Preston. He was ready, therefore, when the Albert Edward Dock was opened on Saturday, the 25th of June and, in fact, played an important part in the events of the day —

On Saturday afternoon, Mr Henry Tyrer, a young shipbroker who had opened an office in Preston shortly before this time, got together a number of men to unload the cargo of the *Lady Louise* and this was the first cargo to be discharged in the dock. The consignment was one of 40 tons and had been specially arranged by Mr Tyrer on behalf of Mr Booth for the opening day and was delivered into the shed in rather less than two hours.[15]

This particular cargo was of provisions from London and was for the account of Messrs E.H. Booth and Company. This was especially appropriate for the senior partner of the firm '. . . was a member of the Town

Council when the Ribble Scheme was first introduced, and it was greatly owing to his advocacy and influence that the vote went in favour of the scheme.'[16]

Tyrer's promising beginning in Preston was followed by further shipments and the Company quickly acquired a dominant position in some trades. In these circumstances a more convenient office was desirable so in May 1893, permission was obtained from Preston Corporation to erect a 'moveable wooden shed' on the South side of the Albert Edward Dock.[17] This was confirmed later in the year when it was agreed that the rent of the site would be £15 per year plus rates.[18] Tyrer's were then well placed to take advantage of the growth in trade which followed the construction of the new dock. Prior to this event, in 1891, imports had amounted to a bare 26,427 tons and exports were only 16,110 tons. By 1894, when the new facility was in full working order, imports had risen to 191,846 tons and exports to 28,313 tons and this dramatic increase was to be maintained so that by 1914 imports totalled 530,251 tons while exports had climbed to 213,339 tons.[19]

The growth of Preston's trade arose for a variety of reasons. The most important items were timber – the first material to be imported in quantity after the new dock was opened: woodpulp which began slowly but became highly significant, and grain which was a traditional import that developed with the improvement to the port's access and capacity. Many other items including petroleum, bitumen, granite, slates and cement helped to swell the totals each year and these were supplemented by general cargoes of groceries, foodstuffs and general merchandise which originated usually in Liverpool and London. The trade with Hamburg resulted in the importation of quantities of sugar and farina[20] but this was handicapped by the lack of return cargoes. Indeed this was a criticism of nearly all of Preston's services as the only significant export was coal and, with the exception of bunkers most of this was directed to the Irish market.[21]

III

As might be expected Henry Tyrer and Company took a very active part in promoting the growing trade of Preston and, on certain routes, established a pre-eminence that was to be of long duration. As in Liverpool the Company undertook a large amount of agency and brokerage work and were appointed to represent both the General Steam Navigation Company and the Ayr Shipping Company. Tyrer's also established a number of regular services to London, Scotland, Hamburg and East

Norway but it was in the grain and, particularly, the woodpulp trades that the Company was to achieve its greatest successes.

The firm of Joseph Pyke and Son, formerly Pyke and Gradwell, had imported cereals from Ireland for many years prior to the opening of the new dock and continued to do so, on a larger scale, when the new facilities were completed.[22] It was then possible to obtain corn, barley and rye from other sources and it seems that Henry Tyrer was instrumental in arranging for supplies to be shipped to Preston from many new areas. Tyrer's original contact with the Pyke family is not known, but it may have been a local recommendation (the Pyke's lived in Preston and Southport) or Tyrer may have undertaken work for Pyke's Liverpool office. Whatever the link, there can be no doubt that by the late 1890s both Edward and Cuthbert Pyke regarded Tyrer as a useful business associate although no evidence has survived of a close friendship.[23]

By the turn of the century Edward Pyke and his son, Cuthbert, were quite wealthy and left the running of their firm to a fellow director, Mr John Hothersall (Senior).[24] They were, therefore, prepared to invest in profitable ventures outside their own particular sphere. Their contact with Henry Tyrer via the importation of grain then provided a common interest and they were happy to join with him in a number of companies where he provided the expertise and they provided the capital. All of these investments were concerned with shipowning and the system that was evolved was designed to give the Pyke's a maximum of collateral. Thus they would acquire only a small number of shares in any new company but would provide substantial capital by financing a mortgage on the vessel itself. Tyrer invariably managed the ships and was able to extend his functions on a scale which would otherwise have been impossible and the Pyke's obtained a good return without becoming involved in any serious risk. Thus both parties were content and the arrangements proved to be long-lasting and mutually beneficial.

The first venture of this nature was in respect of the s.s. *Princess*. This was a small vessel of only 348 tons gross which Tyrer wished to employ in the general cargo trade between London and Preston. He therefore acquired the ship, which was registered as a single-ship limited company (Steam Ship *Princess* Limited) and financed the deal with a £5,750 mortgage at 5½% which was arranged with Joseph Pyke and Son.[25] Tyrer then operated this vessel as intended from April 1899, until some time in 1901 when the *Princess* was sold for £6,000. The company was then placed into voluntary liquidation.[26] The success of this project then led to further co-operation between Edward and

Cuthbert Pyke and Henry Tyrer. This, too, was concerned with the owning and operation of steam vessels but, unlike *Princess*, all future arrangements were to be based on the carriage of woodpulp.

Prior to the improvements to the River Ribble the woodpulp for all the North of England had been imported from Scandinavia via Hull and Goole. Henry Tyrer realised that with the construction of the Albert Edward Dock it would be cheaper to supply the Lancashire paper mills through Preston and, consequently, he is credited with diverting the whole of the woodpulp trade from the East to the West coast.[27] However true this suggestion may be there can be no doubt that the importation of woodpulp into Preston did increase at a really phenomenal rate. Thus while only 595 tons were handled in 1894, by 1915 imports amounted to over 160,000 tons.[28]

Henry Tyrer was active in the woodpulp trade from its inception but, at first, was concerned only with the arrangement of the shipments. His most substantial client was the firm of Becker and Company of 64 Cannon Street, London, and this led to a friendship with its principal, Mr (later Sir) Frederick Becker. As the volume of imports increased, Tyrer chartered many ships specifically for this Company and vessels such as the s.s. *Welhaven*, s.s. *Borg* and s.s. *Peik* operated quite regularly between East Norway and Preston.[29] In these circumstances it seemed to Tyrer that it would be profitable to own, rather than charter, suitable vessels and with this object in mind he approached Becker. Then, after a mutually convenient agreement had been reached, he put the proposition to the Pykes and with their financial backing established a number of small, limited, companies.

The first of these was the Steamship *Prestonian* Limited which was incorporated on 27 July 1899.[30] This was capitalised by the issuing of 1,500 shares of £10 each but the amount that was called up is not known. It was unlikely, however, to have been very much as most of the finance was provided by a £14,000 mortgage taken up by Joseph Pyke and Son. *Prestonian* only operated for a short period and was sold towards the end of February 1900.[31] This would appear to be a most surprising development but the explanation is a simple one. Basically the vessel was not as well suited to the woodpulp trade as had been expected so when a good offer was received it was thankfully accepted and this enabled Tyrer to make other, and better, arrangements.[32]

Tyrer's next step was to organise the Preston Steam Navigation Company Limited, and this was registered on 8 December 1900.[33] The new firm was founded —

to purchase and trade with the s.s. *Hermann*, built in 1890, and for the past two years regularly employed on time charters to Messrs H. Tyrer & Co, and principally occupied in the Preston pulp trade, for account of Messrs Becker & Co, homewards, and in the salt and coal trade outwards.[34]

The strength of the new company lay in the purchase of a vessel[35] that had already proved itself in the trade and in an arrangement made with Beckers that '. . . in consideration of their having the first offer of room in the Steamship, the Company is to have the first refusal of all freights this firm has to offer, suitable for the ship.'[36]

In view of these favourable omens the issue of 600 ordinary shares @ £10 was quickly finalised. Most were taken up by the 'syndicate' – the Pyke's, John Hothersall, Henry Tyrer and Frederick Becker – but about a quarter were sold to the general public. Included in the latter group were many individuals involved in the Lancashire, Westmoreland, Irish and Scottish paper making industries together with several Swedish subscribers. John Porter, Henry Tyrer's father-in-law, also helped by investing in ten shares.[37] The financial arrangements were concluded when Edward Pyke provided a mortgage of £9,000 @ 5½% on the vessel and the administrative system was finalised when Henry Tyrer was appointed as managing director.[38]

The success of the *Hermann* and thus of the Preston Steam Navigation Company Limited, then encouraged Tyrer and the other members of his 'syndicate' to order a new vessel. This was specifically designed to replace *Prestonian* and so was given the same name. *Prestonian* (2) was built by the Ailsa Shipbuilding Company of Troon in 1901 and she was just a little larger[39] than the *Hermann*. The 'syndicate' then ran her for a few months before incorporating a new firm, Steamship *Prestonian* (1902) Limited in March 1902. This Company had many similarities to that set up to operate the *Hermann*. Like the Preston Steam Navigation Company it was managed by Henry Tyrer and enjoyed a similar relationship with Becker and Company. The firm was financed by the issue of 750 ordinary shares @ £10 – 600 of these being reserved for existing shareholders in the Preston Steam Navigation Company – and Cuthbert Pyke provided a £13,000 mortgage @ 5½% which supplied the balance of the purchase price of *Prestonian* (2) which amounted to £19,530.[40]

Details of the workings of this steamer during the period from 17 March 1902 to 30 June 1903, were given by the directors to the first Ordinary General Meeting of Shareholders in August 1903. These showed that *Prestonian* (2) had made gross profits of £1,964 and that after paying all expenses, together with interest and providing for the sinking fund, a dividend of 5% (£375) could be recommended.[41] This was, of course, a reasonable return by the standards of the time but for Henry Tyrer and Company the real returns, both for *Hermann* and *Prestonian* (2) were much greater because of their management agreements.

A third firm to take advantage of Preston's pre-eminence in the woodpulp trade was established by Henry Tyrer on 22 April 1903. This was the Woodpulp Transport Company Limited,[42] and it came into being to provide for the carriage of about 140,000 tons of woodpulp over a seven year period from Canadian ports for the account of Becker and Company. The original contract had been accepted by the Preston Steam Navigation Company, but in view of the very different nature of this business it was decided that a separate concern would be more appropriate.

Once again the 'syndicate' operated in its customary manner. Finance was supplied by 1,000 shares @ £10 of which 750 were reserved for shareholders of either the Preston Steam Navigation Company Limited, or the Steamship *Prestonian* Limited, and Edward Pyke provided a mortgage of £16,000 @ 5½%. These funds were then utilised to purchase the s.s. *Nancy Lee* (formerly s s. *Minterne*) at a cost of £23,800.[43] Henry Tyrer and Company were appointed to manage the vessel which was not only the biggest they had yet had to deal with but also introduced them to deep-sea routes for the first time.[44] This trade also proved to be highly profitable for all concerned but Henry Tyrer's pleasure in this success was marred by an unfortunate investment which he made in the Port of Chicoutimi Limited, a Canadian centre which it was hoped would develop as a major outlet for the export of woodpulp.[45]

IV

The workings of Henry Tyrer's 'syndicate' owed an enormous amount to the financial support provided by the Pyke family. This was covered by individual mortgages on each ship owned by the various firms in which its members were interested but the Pyke's appear to have regarded each transaction as part of a whole. Thus in May 1903, Cuthbert Pyke calculated that he was owed, 'with interest made up to the 29th', the sum of £25,133 6s 3d.[46] The relationship was extremely businesslike and the Pyke's always held the insurance policies which protected the vessels in which they had an investment. The system sometimes worked in reverse and on at least one occasion Joseph Pyke and Son accepted a deposit of £5,000 @ 4% from the Preston Steam Navigation Company — this was is January 1905, presumably just after the *Hermann* had been sold.[47]

This event was a fairly predictable one because by 1905, *Hermann*, built in 1890 was becoming elderly and less efficient. Early in that year, therefore, she was sold and the capital of the Preston Steam Navigation Company was reduced from £6,000 (600 shares @ £10) to only £300 (600 shares @ 10s). This enabled the Company to return £9 10s 0d per share to its supporters and the mortgage held by Edward Pyke was extinguished.[48] A further change came in 1908 when the capital was increased by £7,700 (7,700 @ £1) to make a new total of £8,000.[49] This cash was then used to buy out the shareholders in the Steamship *Prestonian* (1902) Limited and thus the Preston Steam Navigation Company became the owners of *Prestonian* (2) which, of course, continued on her normal route between Preston and Scandinavia.

The pattern of share holdings in the Preston Steam Navigation Company after these events shows that they did not represent any major switch in policy and the 'syndicate' remained in effective control —

Shareholders	*1906*	*1908*
Edward Pyke	100	1500
Cuthbert Pyke	45	500
Henry Tyrer	70	470
John Hothersall	45	500
Frederick Becker	77	910
Joseph Pyke & Son	45	500
Owned by 'syndicate'	382	4380
Other	218	3620
Total:	600	8000

A second change which occurred in 1908 concerned[50] Becker and Company. This was incorporated as Becker and Company Limited, in July 1908, with an issued capital of £100,000.[51] Henry Tyrer took a small share in the new firm which, in spite of its altered status, continued in its traditional trade with little, if any, deviation. Frederick Becker's support for the 'syndicate' also remained unchanged and Henry Tyrer and Company continued to either carry, or arrange, most if not all of his woodpulp cargoes.

V

In the period from 1895 to 1908 Henry Tyrer's business had made great advances and by 1905 his activities at Preston were generating more revenue than those at Liverpool. His importance in Preston can be judged from the way in which he was able to negotiate concessions with the Ribble Navigation authorities. Thus in May 1901, he obtained a major reduction for his London service and this was followed in February 1902 by an agreement for his regular vessels carrying full loads of woodpulp to pay only half dues.[52]

Apart from his particular interest in woodpulp from both Scandinavia and Canada, Tyrer built up his agency business in Preston and established a number of services that, in conjunction with his Liverpool office, provided a comprehensive network that linked many parts of the Continent with London and the north-west ports. These were usually operated with chartered tonnage but, where it seemed profitable, company owned vessels were also utilised. Thus *Princess* was used on the London route while the two *Prestonians*, *Hermann* and *Nancy Lee* — all owned by the syndicate — catered for various aspects of the woodpulp trade. In addition, Henry Tyrer appears to have personally owned two small steamships — albeit with substantial mortgages provided by the Pykes. These were *Duchess*, a small vessel valued at only £3,000 in 1902 and used on coastal routes as demand dictated, and *Fulwood*, valued at £4,000 in 1902[53] and operated in the trade from Liverpool or Preston to Dumfries and Annan.[54]

Henry Tyrer's progress at Preston and his continuing success at Liverpool were complemented by the establishment of a London office in 1900. This was a necessary and desirable event for a number of reasons. In the first place Tyrer's growing involvement with the woodpulp trade at Preston was leading to a strong connection with Becker and Company which had many customers in the London area.[55] Thus the opening of an office in the capital enabled Tyrer to take over the work which had previously been arranged by other firms or by agents acting on his behalf, and he could deal more effectively, and profitably, with cargoes that were partly or wholly consigned to London. A major dispute between Becker and a shipper in respect of a disputed Bill of Lading required an enormous amount of correspondence before it was settled in January 1899, and this may have been of importance in persuading Tyrer that the time was approaching when he needed to set up a permanent establishment in London.[56]

The rising volume of general trade between Preston and London which had led to the employment of *Princess* on this route provided a further incentive for Tyrer to take action and sometime during the Summer of 1900 the matter was discussed with a Mr Theo Van Ishoven. This gentleman had an office at 22 Billiter Street, EC, from where he organised his business as a shipbroker and importer of building materials.[57] He also acted as London Manager for the Compagnie General Maritime Bruxelloise — a Belgian concern, largely controlled by Kortman and Company, which had formerly been known as the Speed Line.

The Company owned two vessels, the s.s. *Alba* and the s.s. *Vanda*, both of 400 net registered tons, which were used to provide a twice weekly service from Brussels to London. They specialised in the carriage of all types of Belgian glass, which was normally in great demand in the British capital, but for reasons which are now not clear, the CGMB decided to re-organise its London terminal. Tyrer's, who had previously utilised the service operated by the Speed Line, were then approached by its London manager who proposed a deal which would have included the chartering or sale of the *Alba* —

With reference to our conversation today. My firm would be prepared to take *Alba* on Time Charter (Government forms) for a period of 6/9/12 months at the rate of £240 per month we having the option of purchasing the Steamer at any time during the existence of the Charter at the fixed price of £7,500.

The customary Commission of 2½% to be paid to my firm on the Charter and in the event of the purchase of the Steamer, a Commission of 1½% to be paid to my firm.

With regard to the Wharf I should be prepared to negotiate with you in respect of the taking over of the premises for the remainder of your lease and, no doubt, this could be arranged. If any advantage to you delivery of the *Alba* could be taken at Antwerp but not before the 1st November, 1900, nor later than the 15th November.[58]

Ishoven quickly replied with a detailed proposal making definite suggestions in respect of the charter or sale of *Alba*. He also asked Tyrer if he would take over the lease of their wharf at Shadwell Basin and of their office in Billiter Street, together with three lighters that were normally used in the trade. He went on —

Regarding the continuation of the service London Brussels we are at your disposal for any information and ask nothing — we pass you the proposed contracts for the handling of glass:

F.W. Fasimiloe Ltd	5s 6d per ton (overside)
George Reginess & Co	6s 6d
Brussels & Co	6s 6d
W. French & Son	6s 6d
Nutting Bros	6s 6d

Plateglass from 14s to 16s per ton domicile, besides that we have a quantity of agreements. Respectfully we beg you to let us know your opinion and idea about the different points related in this letter.[59]

Further correspondence followed and Tyrers obtained full details of freight rates and expenses. A meeting was then arranged between Mr Kortman, the principal shareholder of CGMB and Henry Tyrer after which the latter wrote to the London and India Dock Joint Committee to say that he wished to take over the lease of the 'Brussels Wharf' at Old Shadwell Basin.[60] On the same day, 26 October, Tyrer signed the charter party in respect of *Alba*, made an agreement to charter the three lighters and legally transferred the lease of the wharf. All of these arrangements were confirmed by 'Memorandum of Agreement' made with the CGMB and apart from amplifying many points dealt with elsewhere this also gave Tyrers the lease of the Company's London office.[61]

The effect of this burst of legal activity was that Tyrer secured a complete business together with a wharf, office and ship all without the payment of any premium. The only condition that was imposed was as follows —

This agreement is made in conjunction with Charter of s.s. *Alba* on G.F. Time Charter and is subject to the conditions and stipulations made in that Charter Party (dated 26 October 1900) and this agreement lapses on the withdrawal of the steamer or cancelment of the Charter of the s.s. *Alba* and Henry Tyrer and Company are at liberty to withdraw from the Brussels service whenever and however they may deem it discretionary to do so.[62]

Henry Tyrer and Company duly occupied both the wharf and London office, and began to operate *Alba* under the terms of the chartering agreement. This specifically stated that 'Charterers have the option of running the *Alba* to Preston and Fleetwood twice monthly, that is London to Preston and or Fleetwood thence to London and Brussels with through cargo from and to Preston and or Fleetwood.'[63] It would seem, therefore, that Henry Tyrer had been extremely fortunate in acquiring a business that not only enabled him to diversify without cost but also complemented his existing activities in Preston. It is not clear from the surviving documents, however, if Henry Tyrer ever intended to operate the wharf and its attendant trade or, indeed, if he ever planned to utilise the *Alba* for more than a very short time. The only certainty is that on 3 December 1900, only five weeks after finalising the acquisition of the assets formerly owned by the CGMB, Tyrer agreed to re-sell them.

The new agreement was made with Messrs D.C. Thomas and Sons of 26 Billiter Street, London, who undertook to pay Henry Tyrer, Hornby and Company the sum of £1,400 in return for the transfer of the lease of the wharf at Shadwell Basin and the removal of the *Alba* from the London to Brussels trade.[64] Certain of the provisions of this arrangement were retrospective so it appears likely that once Tyrer had legal possession and clear title he was prepared to sell at once. The only clue to the background to these events is a mention of 'competition' between Thomas and the sailings of the CGMB.[65] The probable explanation, therefore, is that the CGMB would not have been prepared to sell to their competitor and that Tyrer, either knowingly or unwittingly, acted as an intermediary.

Tyrer's firm in these arrangements is known as Tyrer, Hornby and Company. Nothing can be discovered about N. Arthur Hornby except that he was described as a shipbroker of Edendale, Acton,[66] but it is tempting to assume that he played a vital role in the events of October and November 1900. As a London shipbroker he would, perhaps, have known of the competition between CGMB and Thomas and it is possible, therefore, that he suggested the scheme to Tyrer. All that is known for certain is that once the deal had been completed, Tyrer, Hornby and Company of London quickly returned to the customary format of Henry Tyrer and Company.[67]

Whatever the truth of these conjectures the net results were exceedingly satisfactory to Henry Tyrer. He received £1,400 from D.C. Thomas and Company, and although some of this may have gone to N.A. Hornby his total outlay including '½ months hire of s.s. *Alba*' was only £195 6s 8d,[68] although, in fact, he eventually paid £225, 'in full and final settlement of claims as far as we know in respect to wharf arrangements, service of steamer, and in full of Charter Party conditions regarding the withdrawal from the Brussels to London trade . . .'[69]

In addition, Tyrer retained the lease to the office at 22 Billiter Street and this proved to be of such great assistance to his overall business that he maintained a London branch for many years.[70]

Notes

1. See above, Chapter 3, pp. 39-43.
2. Gores' *Liverpool Directory*, 1894.
3. See below, this chapter, pp. 51-2.
4. Gores' *Liverpool Directory*, 1893.
5. *Handy Shipping Guide* (Wilkinson Brothers Limited, London, 30 December 1899), p. 3.
6. See below, this chapter, pp. 53-6.
7. Gores' *Liverpool Directory*, 1894.
8. Ibid., 1896.
9. See below, this chapter, p. 58.
10. Gores' *Liverpool Directory*, 1900. This was at 11 and 12 Salisbury Building, Trafford Road, Salford.
11. See above, Chapter 2, p. 31.
12. Henry Tyrer & Company were UK agents for Richard Hamilton and Son of Philadelphia.
13. Heywood's MSS, Manager's Minute Book, 2A, 10 November 1903, p. 277.
14. Ibid., 4A, 15 January 1906, p. 198.
15. J. Barron, *A History of the Ribble Navigation from Preston to the Sea* (Guardian Press, Preston, 1938), p. 392.
16. Ibid., p. 390.
17. Henry Tyrer MSS, Box 17, Agreement between the Corporation of Preston and Henry Tyrer and Company, 4 May 1893.
18. Ibid., 24 August 1893.
19. Barron, *Ribble Navigation*, 'Abstract Statement of Trade of the Port of Preston since the Corporation became the Sole Owners', see Appendix, Table 3, p. 139.
20. Farina is a kind of flour or meal made from corn, nuts or starchy roots.
21. Barron, *Ribble Navigation*, p. 415.
22. Ibid., p. 414.
23. Henry Tyrer MSS, Box 35. Their extant correspondence is all couched in formal language which showed that a strong trust existed between the parties.
24. Author's discussion with John Hothersall (Junior), 28 March 1978.
25. Henry Tyrer MSS, Box 7, correspondence and receipts between Joseph Pyke and Son and Henry Tyrer and Company.
26. Public Record Office, Kew. Registration Number 56624, BT34: Box 1448. No BT31 is available.
27. *Shipping*, 'Shipping Sidelights', 1 April 1895.
28. Barron, *Ribble Navigation*, p. 411.
29. Henry Tyrer MSS, Box 21.
30. Ibid., Box 14.
31. Ibid.
32. Author's interview with Mr F. Cutts, September 1964.
33. Public Record Office, Kew. File 68156, BT31 – 16538.
34. Henry Tyrer MSS, Box 9, Extracts from the Prospectus.
35. Ibid., Box 15. *Hermann* was of 945 gross tons, 578 net register tons and 1,280 deadweight tons.
36. Ibid.
37. Ibid., Box 9, allotment of shares.
38. Ibid., Box 9, Memorandum of Agreement.
39. Ibid., Box 13. *Prestonian* (2) was 1,152 gross tons, 588 net register tons and 1,580 deadweight tons.
40. Ibid., Box 13, Prospectus.

41. Ibid., OGM, Report of Directors, 13 August 1903.

42. Public Record Office, Kew. File 32720: BT31 – 31883/77090.

43. Henry Tyrer MSS, Box 12, prospectus.

44. Ibid., *Minterne* had been built in 1898 by Short Brothers at Sunderland, and measured 2,823 gross tons, 1,802 net register tons and 4,600 deadweight tons.

45. See below, Chapter 6, p. 91.

46. Henry Tyrer MSS, Box 35, letter from Cuthbert Pyke to Henry Tyrer, 28 May 1903.

47. Ibid., receipt issued by Joseph Pyke & Sons.

48. Public Record Office, Kew. File 68156, BT31 – 16538.

49. Ibid.

50. Ibid.

51. Public Records Office, Kew. File 71816: BT31 – 10970.

52. Henry Tyrer MSS, Box 39, letters from J. Bilsborough, Dock Superintendent, dated 6 May 1901 and 17 February 1902.

53. Ibid., Box 35, insurance policies on *Duchess* and *Fulwood* were held by Joseph Pyke and Son in May 1902.

54. See below, Chapter 5, pp. 68-9.

55. Henry Tyrer MSS, Box 21, letters from Becker and Company refer to Grays Paper Works, McMurrays Royal Paper Mills Limited, and London Paper Mills Company Limited, Dartford.

56. Ibid., correspondence between Becker and Company, and Henry Tyrer and Company in respect of Heen woodpulp ex s.s. *Welhaven*, January 1899.

57. Ibid., Box 10, letter head on correspondence from T.V. Ishoven.

58. Ibid., letter from Henry Tyrer to T.V. Ishoven, 4 October 1900.

59. Ibid., letter from Ishoven to Henry Tyrer, 9 October 1900.

60. Ibid., letter from Tyrer to Dock Committee, 26 October 1900.

61. Ibid., relevant documents.

62. Ibid., Memorandum of Agreement between CGMB and Henry Tyrer and Company, 26 October 1900.

63. Ibid., Charter Party re *Alba*.

64. Ibid., indenture made 3rd day of December 1900, between Messrs D.C. Thomas and Sons and Messrs Henry Tyrer, Hornby and Company.

65. Ibid.

66. Ibid., Hornby signed in this manner on the agreement between CGMB and Henry Tyrer and Company, dated 26 October 1900.

67. Kelly's *Post Office London Directories* show that firm as Tyrer (Henry), Hornby and Company in 1902, but by 1903 it is just Henry Tyrer and Company.

68. Henry Tyrer MSS, Box 10, account submitted by Kortman and Company, 14 November 1900.

69. Ibid., receipt signed by Managing Director of the CGMB dated 18 December 1900.

70. Kelly's *Post Office London Directory*, for 1902, shows that Tyrer had moved from Billiter Street to Hopetoun House, Lloyds Avenue, London EC.

5

THE CHANGE TO 'LIMITED' STATUS

I

By the end of the first decade of the twentieth century, Henry Tyrer and Company were firmly established at Liverpool and Preston and were operating small, but viable, branch offices in Manchester and London. The firm continued to be involved in a whole range of shipping, brokerage and agency business and, as members of a syndicate of Tyrer's friends, operated a number of small steamships. These were employed in the importation of woodpulp, either from Scandinavia or Canada, and were thus part of Tyrer's biggest single interest at this time. It is, of course, difficult to be certain of the balance of Tyrer's affairs in any particular year but, in 1903, he informed his Bank Manager in Liverpool that his turnover at Preston was at least as much as that at his head office.[1] Two years later, when again discussing his affairs with his Liverpool Bank Manager, Tyrer stated —

> . . . that they were doing very well at Preston. Last year [1905] they had 393 steamers consigned to them at Preston, of which over 20 were vessels of over 4,000 tons. Most of their business is now at Preston. Their turnover in their account there is over £100,000 a year. He stated that last year he saved £2,000 after paying all expenses.[2]

That this pattern was maintained during the next few years can be judged by the profits earned by Tyrer's different branches in the year ending 30 April 1915. In this period Liverpool made £500 7s 4d, Preston £1,359 4s 6d and Manchester £33 1s 0d respectively — a total of £1,892 12s 10d.[3] Nevertheless a number of changes did take place in the years preceding the First World War and it is these that must now be examined.

As noted earlier the Preston Steam Navigation Company Limited, had acquired the Steamship *Prestonian* (1902) Limited in 1908.[4] This amalgamation of the 'syndicate's' interests was followed by a similar but much larger consolidation in 1912. The capital of the Preston Steam Navigation Company Limited, was raised to £40,000 at that time in order that it could secure and operate a number of additional steamships. These included the *Nancy Lee* owned by the Woodpulp Transport Company; *Kronprinsesse Louise*, *Elizabeth* and *Gertrude* owned by Becker and Company; and *Gyp* and *Charterhouse* owned by Frederick Becker and all were transferred, in effect, in exchange for shares. This meant that the major shareholders in the Company were as follows —

Shareholders	*18 November 1912*
Frederick Becker	14,557
Becker and Company	2,911
John Hothersall	158
Henry Tyrer	253
Woodpulp Transport Company	10,000
H. & C. Graysons (Shipbuilders)	1,000
	28,879[5]

Thus the 'syndicate' retained a vast majority of the shares of the Preston Steam Navigation Company but the Becker influence was now clearly quite paramount. This was sensible from Becker's point of view as he and his Company provided most of the cargoes which kept these vessels profitably employed. The changes were of little interest to the Pykes who, by then, held only reduced mortgages on *Prestonian* (2) and on *Nancy Lee*, and only token shareholdings in the Preston Steam Navigation Company and in the Woodpulp Transport Company.[6] Henry Tyrer, of course, retained the management of the Company's ships which was his main concern but there can be little doubt that from this time onward he fully appreciated that it was Becker and not he who controlled the policies of the firm.

Becker's increasing interest in the shipment of their woodpulp led to a decreased demand for Tyrer's services in London and in 1913 the office at Hopetoun House was closed.[7] Becker's influence which threatened an important segment of Tyrer's business, could be countered in two ways. In the first place Tyrer ensured that he operated all aspects of the Preston woodpulp business for Becker without criticism and thus gave no cause for complaint which might have been used to suggest unwelcome changes. In the second place Tyrer realised that the long term solution lay in further diversification. He, therefore, sought to expand his other activities and was particularly successful in developing his coastal services from Liverpool to southern Scotland and in continuing to extend his activities on the Preston to London and Preston to Hamburg routes. This policy proved to be so helpful that Tyrer was encouraged to move his Head Office from Rumford Place to 360, Royal Liver Building, Liverpool, during 1913.

Henry Tyrer also attempted to meet the potential loss of his share in Becker's woodpulp trade by entering into an entirely new business. This was signified by the establishment of the Levant Transport Company Limited, which was formed in September 1913.[8] The subscribers included a shipowner (Henry Tyrer), a firm of shipbuilders (H. & C. Grayson) and a fruit merchant (Mr O.K. Freilgrath) and the new firm proposed to take part in the growing importation of fruit from the Near East. For a variety of reasons, the Levant Transport Company does not appear to have actually gone into business. In the initial stages this was probably due to the outbreak of war and then, while hostilities continued, shipping space was not available. Accordingly Tyrer wrote down the value of his shares from £300 to a nominal £20.[9] Conditions when peace returned were very different than when the Company was planned so it went into voluntary liquidation in 1922.[10]

In 1914, however, Henry Tyrer and Company remained a prosperous concern and if a major question mark still hung over Becker's woodpulp trade the measures taken to extend other aspects of Tyrer's activities had been, at least, partially successful. Henry Tyrer had, by then, been in business on his own account for almost thirty-five years and although still a very vigorous man of barely fifty-six he decided that it was time that he gave thought to the future. Without children of his own to succeed him a partnership did not seem appropriate so he took the other most obvious step and made arrangements for his Company to acquire 'limited' status.

II

Henry Tyrer and Company Limited[11] came into being on 9 April 1914, in order to purchase

> . . . the whole of the business connection and goodwill of the Vendor (Henry Tyrer) as a Ship Broker, Ships Agent, Commission Agent and Merchant as now carried on by him at Liverpool, Preston and Manchester but excluding therefrom the business connection and goodwill of the Vendor in and relating to the agencies now held by him for the Netherlands Distilleries, Richard Hamiltons Cooperage, Philadelphia, United States of America, The National Biscuit Company of New York and the Hamburg Bremen Africa Line and Woermann Line Agency but including in the sale the benefit of the contracts entered into between the Vendor and Messrs F.H. Powell and Company Limited and James Little and Company, Glasgow, Limited in the year 1913 so far as the Vendor can sell and transfer such benefit.[12]

It was agreed that the assets to be acquired from Henry Tyrer would be valued as follows: £5,000 was to be paid for goodwill and contracts, £321 8s 5d for furniture and office fittings and £7,917 18s 11d for securities and cash at the bank. The total of £13,239 was to be provided by the issuing of 8,239 ordinary £1 shares and 5,000 £1 cumulative 6% preference shares to Henry Tyrer. Three further ordinary shares were purchased by Tyrer for cash so that he then possessed a total of 8,242 ordinary and 5,000 preference shares.

Henry Tyrer now designated as Governing Director, then allotted one share each to six of his most long serving employees and these were appointed as the Company's first directors.[13] The individuals concerned were Henry E. Drain, Herbert M. Warlow and Thomas Wilson of the Preston Office and Frederick Cutts, James E. Lyon and Walter Stretch of the Liverpool Office.[14] At this stage Henry Tyrer remained practically the sole owner of the new firm but he quickly made arrangements for the directors to be able to qualify for 500 ordinary shares each via a self-financing scheme. This stated that Henry Tyrer should,

> . . . hold five hundred Ordinary shares of one pound each in the capital of the Company subject to the following conditions. The dividend from time to time received on such shares shall be applied in paying to the said Henry Tyrer interest at the rate of 5% per annum on the nominal value of such shares (or of such shares as shall not have been transferred as hereinafter mentioned) and the balance shall be held by the said Henry Tyrer to the credit of the said (*director*) and when the amount standing to his credit shall reach £50 he the said Henry Tyrer will transfer to the said (*director*) Ordinary shares to the nominal value of £50 and so on from time to time until the whole of the said Five hundred shares shall have been transferred. The said (*director*) shall not be entitled to claim or receive in cash any amount standing to his credit but only to a transfer of shares when from time to time the amount of credit reaches £50 . . .[15]

The terms of these agreements forbade the sale of any shares without the consent of Henry Tyrer and provided for their return to the Governing Director at a fair valuation if a director left his employment. These conditions ensured that the share distribution of the Company would remain narrowly based but Tyrer did allow some external investors to take a small interest. Thus in August 1914, he transferred 2,000 preference shares to his wife (hardly an outsider) and 1,500 preference and 800 ordinary shares to H. & C. Grayson Limited, with whom he was on very friendly terms.[16] Then, in November 1916, Tyrer's agreements with his six directors came to fruition and each received the balance of his 500 shares.[17] In itself this could not be expected to widen the Company's share distribution very much as in normal circumstances they could only be re-sold to Henry Tyrer. The only exception to this rule being the right to hand-on shares in the event of death. This was regarded as a very long term possibility but, unfortunately, James E. Lyon was killed in active service whilst serving with the 9th Kings Liverpool Regiment in France,[18] and his shares were then transferred to his widow.[19] The pattern of share ownership was, therefore, marginally altered and this process continued when, many years later, other directors also died. This development was encouraged by further transfers of shares from Tyrer to his fellow directors and to promising employees,[20] some of whom were eventually to be promoted to the boardroom. Nevertheless it is true to say that from the date of incorporation to the present day the pattern of share distribution has remained extremely narrow.

When the 'limited' company was established it did not acquire all of Henry Tyrer's business interests. Some of these like his poultry farm at Rufford and his farm near Llangollen in Wales may best be regarded as hobbies although it is certain that Tyrer hoped that they would pay their way. Another minor interest, which may have been a continuation of a family tradition, was concerned with the cutting of peat. This was obtained from Hoscar Moss on the Burscough to Rufford Road and after drying was sold or distributed via a wholesaler. This activity appears to have continued throughout Tyrer's lifetime but then came to an end.[21] A further number of Henry Tyrer's business activities were specifically omitted from the transfer of his assets and goodwill.[22] These were mainly in the nature of agencies which Tyrer proposed to continue on a personal basis and, in addition, Tyrer owned and operated several other commercial ventures which were not mentioned at all in his agreement with the 'limited' company. Included in this latter group was the '. . . steamer *Fulwood*, the shed at Annan and the investment in the shed at Dumfries together with the equipment at Liverpool, Annan and Dumfries attached to the Liverpool/south of Scotland trade . . .'[23]

Towards the end of 1916 Henry Tyrer decided that he would sell these items to the 'limited' Company and a price of £8,000 was agreed. The purchase was then financed by the issue of 8,000 ordinary £1 shares in Henry Tyrer and Company, Limited, and as this was the time when Tyrer needed to transfer 3,000 shares to his fellow directors

(6 @ 500) it meant that his net total rose by 5,000 shares.[24] It is not certain if the further sale of s.s. *Fulwood* was envisaged when the transfer to the 'limited' Company was arranged but, in the event, it was sold early in 1917 for £9,000 to Messrs Oakley, Sollas and Company Limited.[25] As Henry Tyrer had only valued this vessel at £4,000 in 1902,[26] it is obvious that he had taken full advantage of the wartime rise in ship values. It is equally clear that Henry Tyrer and Company Limited also made a sound purchase for after *Fulwood* had been re-sold they retained a gross profit of £1,000 plus the other items mentioned at Liverpool, Annan and Dumfries.[27]

III

The outbreak of war with Germany on 4 August 1914, marked the beginning of a period of uncertainty for all shipping companies. Tramp chartering and regular sailings both ended and, for a time, many ports were full of vessels awaiting instructions from their owners. The trade of the nation was thus at a standstill but the efforts of the Royal Navy together with the cover provided by the newly organised State Insurance Scheme against war risks rapidly encouraged a return to normal commercial activity.[28]

This is not to suggest that services were once again back to their pre-war state for it took many months to recover from the dislocation engendered by the initial loss of confidence and the subsequent changes in traditional voyage patterns. The ending of trade with Germany caused immense confusion for a while because in 1913 over 3,000 British ships delivered cargoes to German ports[29] and it took time for these to be re-routed or find alternative trades. In general this re-arrangement led to longer ocean journeys being necessary so after a brief period when not all ships could find suitable cargoes the reverse was true and an insatiable demand arose for tonnage to meet the requirements of the armed forces and also to provide the food and materials necessary for the civilian population.

The general disruption was concentrated at certain key ports because the threat of enemy action restricted the use of harbours on the east coast while the Royal Navy requisitioned large areas for its own use in Dover, Liverpool, London, Newhaven and Southampton. In turn these difficulties led to the imposition of surcharges on many freight rates[30] and to the regulation of an ever increasing segment of the shipping freight market. Costs, of course, rose rapidly so in the 'free' sector freight rates escalated to a tremendous extent[31] and the value of un-requisitioned ships increased pro-rata. This became particularly evident

after the Germans intensified their attacks upon British merchant shipping in 1916 and was further intensified when losses reached even
higher levels after the policy of unrestricted submarine warfare was
announced in February 1917. Losses, indeed, became so serious as to
threaten the outcome of the war and it took the introduction of the
'Convoy System', a rigid licensing system that excluded non-essential
imports and massive American construction before the situation could
be brought even partially under control.

The outbreak of war brought an immediate end to Henry Tyrer
and Company's service between Preston and Hamburg and interference
was soon experienced on its Preston to London route. In addition, the
number of vessels arriving from the Baltic and Scandinavia fell quite
sharply so the Company's business at Preston suffered fairly badly.
But Henry Tyrer quickly discovered that the wartime disruption of
shipping provided many opportunities, as well as difficulties, and he
and his Company proved to be so adept at grasping these new developments that the period of war was to prove both busy and profitable.
The adaptability of the firm is easily seen when the results achieved
by Preston, Liverpool and Manchester are compared with the pre-war
position. The situation then was that Preston's profits were nearly three
times those of Liverpool[32] but by 1918 Liverpool's contribution of
£5,529 was more than twelve times that of the £438 achieved at
Preston. Manchester succeeded in earning profits of £254 in that year –
a great improvement on 1914 – but this was not significant as the
office there was regarded as mainly a support for Liverpool and
Preston.[33]

The decline in Tyrer's traditional trades at Preston could not be offset by new activities because the port suffered a catastrophic fall in
both its imports and exports. In 1914 these had amounted to 530,251
tons inward and 213,339 tons outward – by 1919 they had dropped to
82,805 tons and 67,687 tons respectively.[34] Liverpool on the other
hand, showed a tremendous growth in the cargoes it handled[35] so
Tyrer's were able to improve their returns from all aspects of their
agency and brokerage work. The Company continued to cater for most
of its original customers and also gained many more who had been
diverted to the Mersey from their normal peacetime ports. The only
loss of business which Tyrer's suffered at Liverpool was one of their
own choosing and came early in 1917 when the s.s. *Fulwood* was sold
and the south of Scotland service came to a temporary end.[36]

Tyrer's war time results were, of course, achieved in spite of major
staff shortages. The Company was fortunate in having a number of

long-serving men in key positions when the war commenced and, with the exception of Mr J.E. Lyon, all were able to remain at their posts for the duration of the hostilities. It was this group, all of whom became working directors, that carried the burden of extra work at a time when their younger colleagues were away in the armed forces. Additional clerks were recruited but these were liable to volunteer (or be conscripted) when they reached military age so the expedient was adopted of employing four lady typists in the Liverpool office. Of those who joined the services, C. Ford of the Kings Own Royal Lancaster Regiment was killed in France on the same day as Sgt Lyon and the two Alty brothers, Henry and Daniel were both killed in action during the last few months of the war. Those who gave their lives were commemorated by a stained glass window which Henry Tyrer later donated to St James Parish Church at Lathom. Those that survived the war included E.S. Ashcroft, S. Dalzell, A. Elliott, D. Ollerton and G. Sanders and they all rejoined the firm when they were released from the forces during 1919.[37]

IV

So far as Henry Tyrer and Company Limited were concerned the most important single development of the First World War was their appointment as Managing Agents of the Bromport Steamship Company, Limited. This new firm, wholly owned by Lever Brothers, was established in 1916 to help move the stocks of badly needed raw materials which the wartime shortage of shipping was building up in West Africa. It was not Lever's first attempt to enter the West African shipping trade for an earlier venture had been frustrated by the Conference Lines. Now, however, the deferred rebate system lay in abeyance due to the war and the way was clear for a fresh start.

Lever's interests in West Africa began in 1903 when a senior executive, Mr H.R. Greenhalgh, visited the Coast and returned with a favourable report of its potentialities. It was not until 1910, however, that Lever's took any action but then the long-established firm of W.B. MacIver was bought and this was followed, two years later, by the acquisition of Peter Ratcliffe and Company and the Cavella River Company Limited.[38] The particular importance of the purchase of MacIver's was that it brought with it the services of Mr W.K. Findlay who, as noted above,[39] possessed the necessary experience to guide Lever's future development on the coast. It also gave Levers some useful insight into the problems of competing with the shipping conference for MacIvers was virtually alone amongst West African merchants in retaining recent knowledge of chartering to that region.[40]

Lever's then attempted to transform the traditional system of collecting wild fruit and exporting it for processing in Europe, to a plantation production that would utilise modern crushing machinery that operated in West Africa itself. Lever's plans suffered many setbacks on the Coast[41] and costs rose to such an extent that the investment could only be justified if a cheaper method of transporting the finished product could be found. The customary method was by cask but this involved two charges for freight – outward and home – so was quite expensive. The alternative of breaking the barrels down into shooks had the effect of saving freight on the outward voyage but the cost of re-erecting them in West Africa was such that little real advantage was gained. Lever's, therefore, decided to charter a steamship fitted with specially heated tanks which would prevent the palm oil from congealing but the conference lines indicated that if this practice was repeated then Lever's would lose the rebate due on all their previous shipments.[42] At the time Lever's were not prepared to risk a confrontation with Elder Dempster and the Woermann Line so gave up their charter. This made their production uneconomic[43] – their subsidiary, West Africa Oils Limited, lost over £50,000 in 1913 – and consequently they withdrew from this aspect of the trade.

The war with Germany led the Woermann Line to end its services to West Africa and the conference system came to an immediate close. In practical terms this meant that insufficient tonnage was available to lift all the cargoes that were available in spite of the fact that they were given a high degree of priority as being essential to the war effort. Lever's as a major consumer of West African produce, re-opened their mills on the Coast but soon found that sea transport and not production was the limiting factor. In these circumstances it became obvious that the ownership of a small number of vessels would be of great value and thus Lever's decided to establish their own fleet.

At this time the high cost of new tonnage, together with the long order-books of the shipbuilders, encouraged Lever's to seek a ready made fleet. A search for vessels suitable for West African conditions was then undertaken and it was found that Herbert Watson and Company of Manchester were prepared to sell their six existing steamers plus their option on one nearing completion. A deal was quickly arranged and Lever's secured the vessels, complete with the option still building, for the sum of £380,000. Details of the agreement are as follows –

**Ships purchased by the Bromport Steamship Co Ltd, from
Herbert Watson & Co Ltd[44]**

	Name of ship	Gross tons	Year built	Cost to Watsons'	Cost to Levers
1	*Colemere*	2,119	1915	£36,765	£87,000
2	*Delamere*	1,524	1915	27,708	58,500
3	*Flaxmere*	1,524	1915	27,719	58,500
4	*Linmere*	1,578	1913	26,258	57,000
5	*Oakmere*	1,251	1910	19,131	48,000
6	*Redesmere*	2,122	1911	25,644	71,000
	Total purchase price —			£163,225	£380,000

Later, in 1916, Lever's took up Watson's option and acquired the newly built *Eskmere* of 2,292 tons for £68,368 and purchased another vessel — *Rabymere* — of 1,775 tons for £107,750 from Messrs J.C. Gould of Cardiff. The *Kulambangra* of 2,005 tons completed the fleet. This steamship had been built in 1910 for Lever's Pacific Plantations, Limited,[45] but had been brought home when the shipping shortage began to get acute and it was considered that she would be of most value on the relatively short West African route.

While all these arrangements were being finalised the question arose as to who would operate and manage the fleet. It would have been difficult, though not impossible, for Lever's to have set up their own organisation but in the middle of a terrible war they had many other pressing problems to demand their attention and it was much easier to hand the administration over to a completely separate agency. This, of course, was where Henry Tyrer came into the picture and, no doubt, his previous association with Mr Findlay together with his long experience in the West African trade were the deciding factors that secured the appointment for his Company.

Discussions, in fact, took place between Mr H.R. Greenhalgh and Henry Tyrer early in March, 1916,[46] and a provisional arrangement was then reached although the Bromport Steamship Company Limited was not formally registered until 29 April 1916.[47] This agreement was essentially of a temporary nature but was not replaced until 11 June 1917, when a legal commitment was made between Henry Tyrer and Company Limited, and the new line. This appointed Tyrer's as Managing Agents whose duties were

. . . to make the necessary arrangements in connection with the

Entering and Clearing of Ships at the Customs, Securing of Berths, Loading, Discharging, Ordering and Checking Delivery of Stores, Preparation of Manifests and Ships' Papers, Provisioning and Bunkering of the steamers while in Ports of the United Kingdom, Engaging and Signing of Crews, Payment of Allotments of Wages of Crew and Officers, Dealing with Insurance Claims and the performance of such other duties as may become necessary in connection with the management of the steamers' business in the United Kingdom . . .[48]

The agreement fixed the Managing Agent's remuneration at £100 per ship per year plus a commission of 1% on all freight, dead freight and demurrage.[49] The appointment was made for a minimum period that was to end on 30 June 1918, but provision existed for it to continue indefinitely, until one or other of the two parties gave six months notice[50] and, in the event, it was to last for many years.

V

The agreement between Bromport Steamship Company and Henry Tyrer was minuted on the day it was signed, 11 June 1917.[51] It then covered a fleet of eight vessels for *Delamere* had already been lost by enemy action and she was soon to be followed by *Colemere*, *Eskmere* and *Redesmere*. Consequently Tyrer's function as Managing Agents was reduced to taking care of five instead of nine vessels but, even so, it was to make a vital contribution to their earnings –

. . . Although the position of the business with Norway, Sweden and Denmark has been seriously affected by the war, there has been an improvement in other directions. The Company have acted, during the past year, as Loading Brokers and Agents for the Bromport Steamship Co Ltd and not withstanding the large increase which has been necessary in Expenses there remains on the years working, after paying the Governing Directors Salary and Directors Fees, a nett balance of £3,729 2s 6d as compared with £1,115 8s 7d for the previous year . . .[52]

Substantial profits were also earned from this source during the ensuing five years and as earnings at Preston rapidly revived once the war was over, Henry Tyrer and Company Limited achieved exceptionally good results even though the shipping industry was passing through a difficult time.[53]

From Lever's point of view the activities of the Bromport Line were extremely beneficial to the Group as a whole although the loss of four ships always kept capacity at a premium. The sinking of their vessels was particularly unfortunate as Lever purchased three other firms of West African merchants during the war and they placed a further strain on the limited facilities available.[54] In addition, two of Watson's ships had been under requisition when they were acquired by the Bromport Steamship Company and, in May 1917, the remainder of the fleet came under state control. This brought Bromport (and Henry Tyrer's) into close association with Elder Dempster — by far the biggest operators on the route — and with the John Holt Line, for at the government's 'request' they formed an owner's committee '. . . that was designed to ensure that all the tonnage engaged in the trade was allocated in the national interest'.[55]

Thus it was only for the first twelve months of its existence that the Bromport Steamship Company could devote its whole attention to the exclusive carriage of Lever's cargoes but in that period it made a marked contribution to the situation on the Coast —

Our fleet has enabled us to bring from West Africa large quantities of produce that would not otherwise have come forward and that helped our markets generally for raw materials. MacIver's warehouse had been blocked at the time we entered into shipping, but with our ships MacIver's were able to go ahead and buy produce that they would not have been able to buy if we had not had the ships. It had further to be borne in mind that today's prices for the steamers would show a big profit, and in a word, good results have been more real than apparent. On broad principles the steamers purchased had been a great success.[56]

From May 1917, all of the Bromport's vessels were taken over by the Ministry of Shipping at controlled rates and their remuneration and voyage patterns were then decided entirely by the state. In practice, this made very little difference to Lever's as all of its fleet was permitted to remain on the West African run but it meant that in future the Bromport was liable to carry cargoes for other merchants and that Elder Dempster and (to a minor extent) John Holt would continue to ship produce for the Lever Companies. The basis of this arrangement was that all tonnage was to be allocated in proportion to the stocks available for shipment.[57] Lever's thereafter received no special privileges for their cargoes but they gained, as did all the firms engaged in the West African trade, from the additional capacity which the

Bromport Company had brought on to the route.

The benefits obtained by Lever's from the operation of their own vessels poses the question as to why they did not replace their wartime losses and thus make even greater gains? The answer lies in the very high costs of construction or purchase which in 1918 were running at approximately four times pre-war prices.[58] Allied to this was the fear of further losses and the possibility that additional tonnage would have been diverted by the Ministry of Shipping to other trades. Once hostilities had come to an end purely economic criteria was the sole influence on the decision making machinery and the inflated cost of ships in the post-war boom must have been a significant disincentive.[59] Then, by the time that the boom had turned to slump and prices had returned to what was regarded as 'normal', Lever's had undertaken the purchase of the Niger Company and were not prepared or able to consider further capital investment.[60]

During the immediate post-war years, therefore, the Bromport Steamship Company operated its five surviving vessels to carry a substantial proportion of the cargoes of Lever's West African firms which now included the Niger Company. The balance of these shipments was carried by Elder Dempster, the re-organised Woermann Line and a new entrant to the trade, the Holland West Africa Line.[61] By 1923 these companies wished to re-establish a shipping conference on the West African route but they understood that this would not be possible unless Lever's, with its predominant share of cargoes, could be induced to sanction any proposed arrangement.

Lever's financial problems brought on by the acquisition of the Niger Company still continued and with the fall in freight rates there was little incentive to persist in the ownership and operation of their own fleet. Some of Lever's directors, supported and encouraged by Henry Tyrer, thought that the best long-term policy would be to develop the Bromport Line utilising chartered tonnage to save capital if necessary. However, a majority of opinion within Lever's was in favour of ending their own sailings if satisfactory terms could be arranged and this view eventually prevailed. Negotiations with the newly re-established conference then resulted in a guarantee that Lever's cargoes would be carried '. . . at a rate which was to be no higher than that paid by rivals'.[62]

Lever's were satisfied with this undertaking and availed themselves of Elder Dempster's offer to dispose of their now redundant vessels.[63] *Linmere*, *Oakmere* and *Flaxmere* were then sold to McAndrews Limited, and were re-named *Balboa*, *Basan* and *Boscau*. The *Rabymere* was purchased by James Moss and Company and she was re-named *Edfou* — the significance of these particular sales being that they went to lines which were members, like Elder Dempster, of Lord Kylsant's Royal Mail Group.[64]

Henry Tyrer was, of course, deeply disappointed that the Bromport Steamship Company had ended its sailings but was gratified to receive confirmation that this was not because of any fault or omission on his part:

> We had under consideration the Agency Agreement between your-selves and this Company, dated 11th June, 1917, which will auto-matically come to a termination in view of our having sold the whole of our fleet.

> We should like to take the opportunity of expressing our high appre-ciation of the services which you have rendered to the Company and which have given us every satisfaction.[65]

Of more practical compensation to Henry Tyrer and Company was their association with another firm owned by Levers. This was the Southern Whaling and Sealing Company Limited,[66] and Tyrer's had been appointed to be its Managing Agents in 1921. This appointment was not, of course, affected by the demise of the Bromport Steamship Company and so demonstrated that Tyrer's still retained Lever's confi-dence and encouraged the belief that they would receive further com-missions as and when suitable opportunities arose. Little did Tyrer realise at this time that within a very short period he would re-new his connection with the West African shipping trade and that after only a few years it was to present him with yet another major challenge.

Notes

1. Heywood's MSS, Manager's Minute Book, 2A, 10 November 1903, p. 277. Note that Tyrer's bank account at Preston was held by the London, City and Midland Bank Limited.
2. Ibid., 4A, 15 January 1906, p. 198.
3. Henry Tyrer MSS, *Director's Minute Book*, no. 1, p. 10, 30 July 1915.
4. See above, Chapter 4, p. 57.
5. Public Record Office, Kew, File 68156: BT31 — 16538.
6. The Woodpulp Transport Company Limited came to an effective end in 1913 when its remaining assets were purchased by the Preston Steam Navigation Company Limited.
7. Kelly's *Post Office London Directory*, 1914.

8. Public Record Office, Kew. File 131286: BT31 − 21730.

9. Henry Tyrer MSS, *Director's Minute Book*, no. 1, 24 May 1918, p. 34.

10. Public Record Office, Kew. File 131286: BT31 − 21730.

11. Companies Registration Office, London. Live File No. 135181. The Company had a nominal capital of 20,000 ordinary £1 shares and 10,000 £1 cumulative 6% preference shares.

12. Ibid., Memorandum of Agreement between Henry Tyrer and Henry Tyrer and Company Limited, 1 May 1914.

13. Ibid., Return of Allotments, 1 May 1914.

14. Ibid., Report under Companies Acts, 1 May 1914.

15. Ibid., Memorandum of Agreement between Henry Tyrer and James Edward Lyon (director), 27 April 1914.

16. Henry Tyrer MSS, *Director's Minute Book*, no. 1, 21 August 1914, p. 6.

17. Ibid., 16 November 1916, p. 20.

18. Ibid., 15 August 1917, p. 32.

19. Ibid., 24 May 1918, p. 35.

20. Ibid., 23 December 1966, p. 23. This refers to the transfer of 100 ordinary shares from Henry Tyrer to James Watson.

21. Discussion with J. Lea, 9 November 1978.

22. See above, p. 66.

23. Henry Tyrer MSS, *Director's Minute Book*, no. 1, 16 November 1916, p. 19.

24. Ibid.

25. Ibid., 26 May 1917, p. 27.

26. See above, Chapter 4, p. 58.

27. The agreement also included the transfer of five 4% debenture bonds of £50 each in the Nith Navigation Commission.

28. C.E. Fayle, *The War and the Shipping Industry* (Oxford UP, London, 1927), pp. 46-67.

29. Ibid., p. 37.

30. C.E. Fayle, *Sea Borne Trade*, vol. 1 (John Murray, London, 1920), p. 191.

31. Fayle, *The War and the Shipping Industry*, p. 440.

32. See above, p. 64.

33. Henry Tyrer MSS, *Director's Minute Book*, no. 1, 24 May 1918, p. 34.

34. J. Barron, *A History of the Ribble Navigation from Preston to the Sea* (Guardian Press, Preston, 1938), p. 409; see Appendix, Table 3, p. 139.

35. S. Mountfield, *Western Gateway: A History of the Mersey Docks and Harbour Board* (Liverpool University Press, 1965), p. 205; see Appendix, Table 5, p. 141.

36. See above, pp. 68-9.

37. The Company helped to make up the wages of those serving in the forces and provided either a pension or a lump sum for the relatives of those killed in action.

38. P.N. Davies, *The Trade Makers: Elder Dempster in West Africa, 1852-1972* (George Allen and Unwin, London, 1872), pp. 178-81.

39. See above, Chapter 3, pp. 45-7.

40. Ibid.

41. C. Wilson, *The History of Unilever* (Cassell, London, 1954), Book 1, p. 181.

42. Committee on Edible and Oil Producing Nuts and Seeds, HMSO, 1916, Cmnd 8248, Q 2646-7.

43. Ibid., Q 2596.

44. *Fairplay*, 20 April 1916, p. 644. See also *Fairplay*, 25 May 1916, p. 810 and 15 June 1916, p. 921.

45. Wilson, *The History of Unilever*, p. 163.

46. Henry Tyrer MSS, Box 25, correspondence between Henry Tyrer & Co Ltd, and Lever Brothers Ltd (O & F Department) 3 and 6 March 1916.

47. File 143730, Dissolved Company file retained at Companies House, City Road, London.

48. Henry Tyrer MSS, Box 25, Agreement dated 11 June 1917, between Henry Tyrer and Co Ltd, and the Bromport Steamship Co Ltd, section 3.

49. Ibid., section 4.

50. Ibid., section 9.

51. Ibid., *Director's Minute Book*, no. 1, 11 June 1917, p. 28.

52. Ibid., 28 June 1917, p. 29. Lever's were aware of Tyrer's profits so while the provisional agreement of 1916 gave their Agents 1½% commission this was reduced to 1% in the permanent arrangement of 1917.

53. See below, Chapter 6, p. 80.

54. These were John Walkden and Company, the Bathurst Trading Company and Kings of Bristol.

55. Davies, *The Trade Makers*, p. 202.

56. C.C. Knowles Esq, of Lever Brothers Limited, speaking in October 1917. Quoted in Wilson, *The History of Unilever*, pp. 238-9.

57. *Fairplay*, 13 June 1918 (AGM of Elder Dempster & Co Ltd), pp. 102-8.

58. *Fairplay* provides details each year of the 'Cost of a new ready steamship of 7,500 gross tons', which is an excellent guide to annual fluctuations.

59. Ibid.

60. Wilson, *History of Unilever*, pp. 252-9.

61. The Holland West Africa Line had gained a footing in the trade during the war when Holland was neutral and the conference system was inoperative.

62. Davies, *The Trade Makers*, p. 221.

63. *Kulambangra* had previously been sold to the Limerick Steamship Co Ltd.

64. P.N. Davies and A.M. Bourn, 'Lord Kylsant and the Royal Mail', *Business History*, vol. XIV, no. 2, July 1972, p. 108.

65. Henry Tyrer MSS, Box 25, letter from N. Charles Watt, Managing Director of the Bromport Steamship Co Ltd, 7 September 1923.

66. See below, Chapter 6, pp. 86-8.

THE INTER-WAR YEARS

I

The ending of the war with Germany in November 1918, saw Henry Tyrer and Company Limited, firmly established on sound foundations. All employees who had served in the Armed Forces could, therefore, be re-engaged without difficulty but this led to a re-organisation under which two of the lady typists lost their positions.[1] Tyrer's work on behalf of the Bromport Steamship Company was then providing the bulk of the firm's income but the woodpulp trade at Preston rapidly revived — partly because of Tyrer's policy[2] — and by 1920 was again making a larger contribution to revenue than Liverpool.[3] Thus the early post-war period proved to be extremely profitable for the Company and it was not until 1924 that results were disappointing and even then they were double those of 1914-15.[4]

Nevertheless, it is certain that throughout these years of prosperity Henry Tyrer felt that it was unwise to rely too heavily on either wood-pulp (with its strong dependence on Becker and Company) or on the Bromport Line (with its policy dictated by the interests of the Lever Group). In the light of subsequent events it is easy to suggest that Henry Tyrer 'knew' that both of these cornerstones of his firm's success would soon disappear but it is more likely that in the very difficult days of the early 1920s he was merely being prudent. There can be no doubt, however, that Tyrer did attempt to diversify very strongly during this period and it is these events that must now be examined.

Even before the war had ended Tyrer had approached Canadian Pacific Ocean Services Limited, and had been appointed as their Liverpool passenger agents.[5] He had also made an agreement with Joseph Sankey and Sons, Limited, for the supply of steel casks to a number of important West African merchants[6] thus indicating that his wartime concentration on shipping was not to interfere with his traditional agency business on the Coast. Tyrer obviously attached considerable significance to his original activities in Liverpool so, when the opportunity arose, he was prepared to dispose of his Manchester office in the overall interest of his Company. The profits from this supporting branch had risen encouragingly during the war but when an advantageous offer was made by the Thoresen Line, Tyrer did not hesitate and it was sold in January 1920. Tyrer's then received £1,000 in cash and £500 in shares but the

1. Ormskirk Station, c. 1890

2. s.s. *Prestonian* (II)

3. James Edward Lyon, Senior, member
of original Board of Directors

4. Thomas Wilson, Governing Director 1936–45

5. John Wilson, nephew of Henry Tyrer, died in West Africa April 1904

6 Henry Tyrer c.1908

S.S. Prestonian
Forcados
10/4/04..

Messrs Henry Tyrer
— ?
Dear Sir,

No doubt you will
have heard the dreadful news from Lagos
which happened at Capetown April 9
5.30 pm. Mr Wilson & Mate & I went to bathe
among the logs where all hands had been
bathing all day. I did not get into the water
at all & was pilot-watching myself. Mr Wilson
& 2 male were swimming & when suddenly Mr
Wilson threw up his hands towards my gang
& failed. also Mr Peel & mr dived down all
over & could see nothing, extract? The depth of
water was 17 feet - Poor Izreck up the river
about one hour later a woman was drowned! —
Its awful sad. I feel for you all, as the heart
of family's sake that on Tuesday 5 to a native

brought the body to Gabeloum, he saw an Alligator
trying to take the body to the bush. Well all Imian
was paid by every one to Mr Ramauos & honed about
¼ mile from Mr Neil house. Poor man, like he has been
an awful shock to us all. Mr Izreck went to Lagos
by Father & was to see you he had news he promised to
write at Lagos till I came back me to square up all
the business. Mr Izreck is a Gentleman — I am now
nearing Forcados I will clear from here to-day
for Lagos, it will clear Lagos to-morrow. I shall write ?
also write him Lagos & give you more news...I have a fine
cargo. My two male was ok daily. 2 Mate is now over
a week & Mate — he is putting up Mork, that the boys
I think he will soon be all right-again. I for now
has had fever, all went well I'm good Spirit- till this sad
event. finally Mr Tyrer don't know what to say, but will
explain better on arrival home, all papers theirs are right
Tell in effect- those locked I will sort all, till ship gets
to home. I & and Poor Izreck for you, & but-now have
got over the shock, I will look after my duty I'm interested
I shall work & coal at Forcados. Now, you all have all the
time. Tray own sympathy, for we all had the
greatest-respect-for him.   I am, dear Sir

Your Obedient-Servant-
William Ker, Master.

8.   Silver rose bowl presented to Henry Tyrer on his 50th Birthday by the Staff of his Preston Office, 2 March 1908

9. s.s. *Congonian* (ex *Quercus*), owned and operated by the United Africa Company in the 'Thirties'

10. Frederick Cutts, Chairman and Managing Director, 1945–68

11. Staff of Preston Office, c. 1928

12.   The Staff at 'Bewcastle', June 1935

13. Henry and Jane Elizabeth Tyrer on their Golden Wedding
Anniversary, June 1935

14. Henry Tyrer in his rose garden at 'Bewcastle' towards the end of his life

15. Seaforth Timber Terminal, Liverpool: on the left m.v. *Cedrela* of East Asiatic Co, Copenhagen and on the right m.v. *Benlawers* of Ben Line Ltd, Edinburgh

16. Tyrer Transport Services Fleet

17. Haulage Depot Staff and Vehicles

18. The Staff, January 1979

19.   Directors and Secretary January 1979. Left to right: B. Dowd (Secretary), G.B. Hannan, G.E. Stretch, J. Lea, C.W. Harrison (Chairman), R. Kaye, J.F. Sanders, D.C. Harrison

20.   Charles W. Harrison, present Chairman and Managing Director

real value of the deal was that they secured the Agency at Liverpool for all of Thoresen's vessels.[7]

Henry Tyrer also strengthened his position at Liverpool by deciding to undertake his own stevedoring. Until 1919 Tyrer's had used Messrs Coggin and Griffiths for this work but thereafter it was performed by a new company especially created for the purpose. This was Freight Conveyors Limited[8] and besides Henry Tyrer the subscribers (and subsequent shareholders) were Samuel Greenhalgh and his son, Henry Jimpson Greenhalgh. The former was a cousin of Mr H.R. Greenhalgh of Lever Brothers and the latter (who was appointed to be the firm's first Managing Director) further improved the Lever connection by arranging for his cousin, Mr J.K. Greenhalgh, to become company auditor.[9] Henry Tyrer might have hoped that these links would have assisted in cementing the friendly relationship that existed between Levers and himself. It may well, in fact have achieved this object but, in addition, it proved to be highly profitable and also enabled Henry Tyrer and Company Limited to offer an even wider range of services to its customers.

Another, less successful, attempt at diversification resulted in the formation of Tyrer's Coasters Limited.[10] This was registered in March 1920, and 19,240 shares of £1 (10s called) were issued. Amongst the shareholders were Henry Tyrer (1,000), J.E. Tyrer (500), Cuthbert Pyke (2,000) and W.K. Findlay of the Niger Company (1,000).[11] Tyrer was made Managing Director (Pyke was the only other director) and the object of the firm was to construct and operate a number of concrete barges and coastal steamers.[12] Tyrer had apparently been impressed by the concrete barges used by the Liverpool Grain Storage Company during the war so when he heard that a Preston shipyard,[13] which had begun the construction of two small concrete coasters, was in trouble he thought that this was a good opportunity to extend his interests. Unfortunately, the one vessel that was completed, the s.s. *Burscough,* proved to be so underpowered as to be unpractical and after only a single trial voyage she was sold and was eventually used as a jetty in the Isle of Man.[14] The other coaster was never finished and the firm went into voluntary liquidation in March 1925.[15]

Henry Tyrer had been concerned with the provision of coal for his clients at Liverpool for many years but it was not until the post-war fuel shortage that he decided to provide the same service at Preston. In March 1920, the Coal Controller imposed the same restrictions on Preston as already existed for Merseyside so that —

... all bunker coal be imported from South Wales and that no bunkering be done from Lancashire Coal. Henry Tyrer & Co Ltd are the principal firm of shipowners and brokers at Preston and, in the interest of their numerous Shipping friends they have decided to undertake the importing and shipping of Welsh coal.[16]

Tyrer prudently obtained an undertaking from the Coal Controller that the order would not be withdrawn without giving him sufficient notice to clear out any stocks of Welsh coal before Lancashire supplies were again permitted.[17] Thus Tyrer's enterprise provided a valuable service to vessels calling at Preston and the Company earned useful revenue without any risk. This development was, of course, only a short-term arrangement that quickly ended: of much more lasting significance was Tyrer's appointment as Managing Agents for the Southern Whaling and Sealing Company Limited.

At the end of the First World War Lever Brothers were the world's largest consumers of whale oil. Much of this was obtained from the Southern Whaling and Sealing Company Limited, which had been founded by Irvin and Johnson (steam fishing vessel owners) of North Shields in 1911.[18] The firm operated a land station in South Georgia together with a number of whale 'catchers' and two tankers which were used to bring the oil to Britain. For reasons best known to themselves Lever's decided to purchase this Company and as Henry Tyrer's were managing their Bromport Line quite successfully it seemed logical to use them in the new venture. Accordingly, in March 1921 an agreement was signed between Henry Tyrer and Company and the Southern Whaling and Sealing Company and this fixed payments as follows: 'The remuneration to be paid to the Agents will be the sum of £1,500 p.a. payable quarterly, but if the present fleet is increased the Agents remuneration to be proportionately increased also.'[19]

Fortunately for Tyrer's the growth of the trade and the changing technology employed meant an increasing use of 'factory' ships so their work grew quite rapidly. Thus in 1921 Tyrer's looked after ten steamers for the Company but by 1924 the fleet had risen to sixteen vessels. This led to their remuneration being increased to £2,250 a year and in 1929 this figure was raised again to £3,000.[20] These receipts went a long way towards offsetting the loss of income caused by the demise of the Bromport Steamship Company[21] and then helped to reduce the disappointment created by the liquidation of Becker and Company.

II

The re-organisation of the Preston Steam Navigation Company in 1912[22] left it in the effective control of the Becker family and, in 1916, Henry Tyrer ceased to be a director of the firm he had done so much to establish.[23] The undertaking remained profitable until the post-war slump but then it quickly got into difficulties. This was because its principal activity, the carriage of woodpulp for Becker and Company, no longer provided an easy living. In an attempt to improve efficiency, therefore, the Preston Steam Navigation Company and Becker and Company amalgamated their interests — the assets of the former being acquired in exchange for shares in the latter.[24] Unfortunately this action proved to be insufficient and in 1924 Becker and Company went into voluntary liquidation.

A new firm, Becker and Company (1924) Limited, was subsequently organised to acquire the assets and business of the original concern and thus Henry Tyrer lost only part of his investment at this time.[25] Nevertheless the impact of this event led Tyrer's to examine the whole range of their holdings in other companies —

> The Directors have pleasure in reporting that the years working has again been satisfactory, but owing to the unfortunate failure of Becker & Co Ltd, and associated companies, in which this Company held a large number of Shares, the Directors have thought it the wisest course to write off, not only the Debts owing, but also the value of all Shares, which are held to be of doubtful value.[26]

The consequence of this decision was that the net profit of £9,906 9s 8d had to be reduced by £1,038 2s 9d to allow for bad debts and by £5,437, the value of shares written off, so this left only £3,431 6s 11d to be transferred to the Profit and Loss Account.[27] In addition, the amount of work undertaken by Tyrer's for Becker and Company (1924) Limited was greatly reduced and even this came to an end when it ceased trading in 1931.[28] This is not to suggest that Tyrer's interest in woodpulp was terminated — the Company continued to act for other firms for many years — but a major source of revenue which had proved of great value to Henry Tyrer in his early days at Preston was no longer available.

In a short space of time, therefore, Henry Tyrer and Company had lost what had been two of their most important activities — the Agency of the Bromport Line and the woodpulp business of Becker and Company — and a further difficulty developed during the same period. This was concerned with the decision to open a new office in London for premises had been acquired at No 11, Great St Helens, in August 1922.[29] It was anticipated that this would facilitate the chartering undertaken by the Company and shares were accordingly secured in the Baltic Merchant Shipping Exchange.[30] Unfortunately the London branch did not prove viable and after losing £1,725 in 1923[31] and a further £775 in 1924[32] it had to be closed.[33]

III

The distressing events described above had already been partly offset by Tyrer's attempts to enter new trades and the Agency for the Southern Whaling and Sealing Company was providing some valuable compensation for losses suffered elsewhere. A further step forward was achieved in 1924 when Henry Tyrer and Company obtained the Preston Agency for Coast Lines Limited, and for the British and Irish Steam Packet Company Limited. It seems probable that the Company secured this very welcome work because of the long-standing friendship between Sir Alfred Reed, Chairman of these cross-channel lines, and Henry Tyrer but the occasion for their Agreement[34] was the shipowner's decision to close their office at Preston.

Tyrer's were appointed, therefore, to deal with the very considerable trade that existed between Dublin and Preston. It was arranged that they should receive 5% commission on the net sea freight for general cargo and livestock and 2½% on cement. In return Tyrer's agreed to pay £400 for the building, furniture and cattle gangways which the ship-owners had previously used at Preston and undertook to take over the lease for the land on which these premises stood on the South side of the Albert Edward Dock. Tyrer's also promised to close their London Office and to transfer to Coast Lines and the British and Irish Lines, '. . . all and every business in London of which they have at present control . . .'[35]

The Agreement was for an indefinite period but could be terminated by either party giving six months notice. Tyrer's seized this opportunity with both hands and gave such great satisfaction to their clients that in 1928 they were awarded, '. . . a further fixed sum of £100 p.a. . . .'[36] and the relationship continued to prove mutually beneficial until circumstances were completely changed in the post-war era.

Henry Tyrer's service to southern Scotland also proved viable in the 1920s and 1930s. This utilised chartered tonnage to carry animal feeding stuffs from firms such as Bibby's, Silcocks and Calthropes, sugar from Tate and Lyle and groceries from Travers between Liverpool and Annan,

Dumfries and Kirkcudbright. During this period rail costs would have averaged about 25s per ton but Tyrer's could move these items for only 10s to 12s per ton.

Tyrer's operated from an appropriated berth at South No 2 Huskisson Dock[37] and, after advertising a sailing to coincide with the Scottish tides, would charter a suitable vessel from a local firm like Monks or Monroe, or perhaps from the Ramsey Steam Ship Company with whom a special relationship appears to have developed. A typical arrangement would be to pay about £60 for the trip which would include 48 hours for loading and discharging.[38] The trade was facilitated by Tyrer's ownership of a 'Shed' at Annan and by renting a store at Kingholm Quay, Dumfries, from the Nith Navigation Commissioners.[39]

The business continued up to 1939 but was not re-started after the war because road transport had so improved that ships could only compete with full loads and even this activity gradually came to an end. For a while, however, many cargoes of grain were shipped to southern Scotland — a major customer being James Derby of Castle Douglas who imported maize into Kirkcudbright where they had a plant for making 'UVECO' cattle cake.[40]

Tyrer's attempts at diversification achieved a further success when, in 1925, the Company was appointed Liverpool Agents for the Jaffa Union Line.[41] They also consolidated their position as agents for the Netherlands Distilleries by negotiating an agreement with H.B.W. Russell and Company Limited, in respect of the 'Camel' trade mark claimed by both in Nigeria and the Gold Coast.[42] This generated extra business which required additional storage space so two extra rooms were leased in Royal Liver Building close to the firm's main offices.[43]

Taken together Henry Tyrer's other activities at Liverpool and Preston were profitable enough to easily overcome the losses and disappointments suffered through the ending of the Bromport Agency and the termination of the relationship with Becker and Company. Indeed, Tyrer's general progress at this time was so marked that special arrangements had to be made with his Liverpool Bank in order to provide additional credit facilities. This was because of the need to pay for bunkers and other expenses[44] incurred on behalf of clients which rose to such an extent that the Company deposited its War Stock so as to obtain a further £5,000 overdraft without the use of any special guarantees.[45] Henry Tyrer then attempted to consolidate his success by arranging for two of his directors to visit the Company's contacts abroad. Thus in the winter of 1924 Mr Cutts was sent to the United States and Canada while Mr Wilson travelled to Norway, Sweden, Finland, Denmark,

Germany and Holland.[46] Both were extremely well received and this encouraged Tyrer to express his confidence in the future by purchasing an additional plot of land at Preston.[47] This was sited at Watery Lane and was acquired in case the Company wished to expand its operations at that port[48] but, in fact, the next major development was to be Tyrer's re-entry into the West African shipping trade and this was a purely Liverpool affair.

IV

The loss of the Bromport Line Agency had come as a great shock to Henry Tyrer for he had regarded this venture as most successful from every point of view. He appreciated that the sailings had been terminated in what was considered to be the overall interest of the Lever Group and was reassured that no blame attached to him by his continuing work for the Southern Whaling and Sealing Company. Nevertheless, and in spite of the fact that his other activities quickly filled the financial gap, Tyrer deeply regretted that his expertise in West African shipping was not being properly exploited. Consequently he approached the African and Eastern Trade Corporation and they eventually agreed to give his proposals a practical test.

The African and Eastern had been established in 1919 by the amalgamation of four important firms of West African merchants.[49] These were the African Association Limited, F. & A. Swanzy Limited, Millers Limited and Miller Brothers (of Liverpool) Limited and together they formed a group that was almost as large as that controlled by Lever Brothers. In October 1920, Lever attempted to combine his interests in West Africa with those of the Corporation but although it was welcomed by the shareholders the scheme did not go ahead because of the world slump and the financial difficulties of the Lever empire.[50] As a result the two 'giants' of the West African merchanting trade continued to operate independently and each made its own arrangements for the shipment of its cargoes. Up to 1923 the Bromport Steam Ship Company carried most of the goods and produce of the Niger Company and other Lever firms. This was, of course, known to the Directors of the African and Eastern but at a time when freight rates were low and shipping abundant they took no steps to organise their own independent line. The setting up of the West African Lines Conference then led to the end of the Bromport's sailings and to the regulation of the trade. The African and Eastern up to this date had shipped their cargoes via Elder Dempster and the Woermann Line and acquiesced with the new arrangement on condition that the freight rates they were charged were no higher than those paid by their rivals. With a suitable assurance from WALCON all of the African and Eastern's business continued to be handled by the conference and, but for the intervention of Henry Tyrer, it is likely that the situation would have remained unchanged for many years.[51]

The demise of the Bromport Steamship Company meant a loss of revenue and pride to Henry Tyrer but to the officers and crews of its vessels it meant the loss of their livelihood. Some were able to remain in their ships when they were acquired by the Royal Mail Group, but a large number were left without employment and this provided Tyrer with yet another incentive to approach the African and Eastern Trade Corporation. Tyrer's experience in the West African shipping trade then enabled him to convince the directors that it would be profitable for them to have their own vessels and this, combined with the unease created by the re-introduction of the deferred rebate system, persuaded them to agree to the purchase of a single, very old, vessel. However Tyrer was then able to explain to the Corporation that at least two ships were desirable to offer anything like a service and it was finally agreed that two suitable steamers be acquired.

The first of what was to become a substantial fleet was *Fordefjord,* a Norwegian shelter decker of 2,116 gross tons. This cost approximately £24,000[52] which was a moderate price for a vessel built only seven years earlier but the second purchase, *Commodore,* although slightly larger had been constructed in 1900 so cost only £7,442.[53] These ships were re-named *Ashantian* and *Ethiopian* respectively and they proved to be such an immediate success that Tyrer had little difficulty in persuading the African and Eastern to purchase additional tonnage. In 1925, there-fore, a new ship — the *Nigerian* of 3,543 gross tons — was constructed by Messrs Barclay, Curle and Company of Glasgow at a price of £70,299.[54] The service was then augmented by *Woodville*[55] which although elderly gave satisfactory help until 1928 when a second new vessel, *Lafian,* was obtained from Barclay, Curle for £80,588.[56]

Thus from 1925 to 1929 the African and Eastern Trade Corporation owned four vessels: *Ashantian, Ethiopian, Nigerian* and either *Woodville* or *Lafian* and these were able, together with a judicious amount of chartering at seasonal peaks, to carry most of its cargo. The balance, particularly urgently needed items, was shipped by the Conference Lines at tariff rates with the understanding that the Corporation would not pay more than its competitors for this service.[57] This arrangement proved to be quite successful and Henry Tyrer's forecasts were fully vindicated. One example of this can be shown by *Ethiopian* which although she had cost only a minute sum in 1925 made a net profit of nearly £6,000 on a single voyage in 1927.[58] The *Nigerian* was, of course, much more expensive but she quickly proved her worth by making a net profit of over £9,000 on one of her early trips.[59] Returns such as these could not be concealed for long and after making suitable enquiries Lever Brother's decided to re-enter the shipping business. This was undertaken on a very modest scale – a single, ancient, ship the *Ars* being purchased for about £8,000 in 1928 – but when she paid for herself in less than two voyages Lever's began to take a much more serious interest in the West African shipping trade.[60]

Evidence of the profitability of shipowning came at a crucial stage in Lever's re-organisation of its West African interests. As noted above[61] Lever's had failed in an attempt to amalgamate their Merchanting firms on the Coast with the African and Eastern Trade Corporation in 1921 and so throughout the 'twenties the two groups had continued to exist and competed vigorously for the available business. In 1928, however, the African and Eastern Trade Corporation got into financial difficulties so after much negotiation it and the Niger Company ceased trading and transferred their fixed and floating assets to a new firm, the United Africa Company, Limited.[62]

V

The first chairman of the United Africa Company was Sir Robert Waley Cohen and he was responsible for many of the decisions that were necessary to develop a single, new, organisation. Cohen had at one time been a Managing Director of Shell Transport and Trading Company Limited,[63] so although trained as an accountant he also had a useful knowledge of shipping. Consequently he took an active interest in negotiating freight rates with the West African Shipping Conference and argued that in view of the very substantial cargoes provided by the Niger Company and the African and Eastern in 1928 that the UAC should enjoy preferential terms.[64]

In his discussions with WALCON Cohen pointed out that it cost 45s per ton to ship with them whereas his own vessels, organised by Henry Tyrer's could transport cargoes to and from West Africa at only 25s 6d per ton. The Conference, led by Elder Dempster, agreed to reduce their rates by enough to satisfy Cohen but insisted that the reductions be available to all shippers. This did not suit Cohen and, eventually, it proved to be impossible to find a compromise and the UAC decided to carry all of its cargoes in its own or in chartered vessels.[65]

Henry Tyrer and Company had, of course, assiduously encouraged the UAC to break with WALCON and on 29 August 1929, had sent a comprehensive analysis of the situation to Cohen entitled, *Carriage of Merchandise and Produce to and from West Africa.*[66] This document claimed that it would be easy to provide alternative services at moderate rates without large capital expenditure and Cohen was so impressed that he authorised Tyrer's to prepare plans for any eventuality. Thus when negotiations finally collapsed it was only necessary to send a telegram to Tyrer's and the appropriate machinery was set in motion.[67]

As already noted,[68] part of the UAC's cargo was carried during 1929 by the five vessels previously owned by the African and Eastern, and the Niger Company. Two additional ships *Mendian* and *Zarian,*[69] were purchased in 1930 but as the *Ars* was sold the net increase in capacity was very small. Tyrer's filled the gap between what this Company owned fleet could carry and what was required by making full use of chartered tonnage and by the end of January 1930, thirty-seven vessels had been fixed through Messrs Erlebach and Company.[70]

During the remainder of the 1930s Tyrer's continued to arrange for the shipment of practically all of UAC's West African cargoes. At first the proportion of Company owned vessels was small but the fleet, after experiencing very slow growth until 1935, was then rapidly expanded so that chartering was only necessary at seasonal peaks or for other special reasons —

Growth of the UAC Fleet[71]

1929	15,166 gross tons	1935	28,935 gross tons
1930	19,797	1936	56,391
1931	23,197	1937	77,045
1932	22,679	1938	81,916
1933	29,781	1939	81,916
1934	29,871		

The sudden growth of Company owned tonnage in 1936 came about as a result of the changing policy of Lever Brothers which, in turn, was dictated by the overall interests of the Group. The underlying factor which influenced this change was the pattern of Lever's trade with Germany for this had resulted in the building up of large balances of blocked marks.[72] Under German regulations these could only be spent within the country so Lever's devised a plan to purchase a number of trawlers, tramps, tankers and whale catchers which were to be constructed in German yards.[73] Altogether over 300,000 gross tons were acquired under these arrangements and the UAC received eight vessels totalling 42,524 gross tons during 1936 and 1937.

There is no evidence to suggest that either the UAC or Henry Tyrer and Company ever requested a share in the German built tonnage for use on West African routes but it seems certain that both parties were happy to operate the new ships when they became available. In the first instance the increase in the size of the UAC fleet was offset by the sale of four of the older units but criticism of Lever's for building in Germany at a time of high unemployment at home then led to further ships being ordered. Thus an additional six vessels were constructed in British yards and it was when these joined the service that Company owned tonnage rose so dramatically.[74]

So far as Henry Tyrer and Company were concerned these developments provided welcome extra work although their activities in the charter market were substantially reduced. Indeed, the organisation of the UAC's shipments became Tyrer's principal business and, as trade recovered from the very low levels of 1931[75] volume increased and this led to a further large rise in shipments and revenue.

VI

The success of Henry Tyrer and Company in overcoming the difficulties created by the post-war slump in trade was an immense achievement and owed a great deal to the inspiration and drive of the firm's Governing Director. By 1920 Henry Tyrer was approaching his mid-sixties but was still in vigorous health and in full control of the Company. Thus he was responsible for the policies which enabled the firm to survive the loss of the Bromport Agency and the collapse of Becker and Company at a time when the entire shipping industry was in disarray.[76] Henry Tyrer's experience in building up his business from nothing led him to appreciate, better than most, that the agencies he operated were very tender 'plants' which required constant attention and which, in spite of every effort, might wither and die. Accordingly, be made every effort to broaden the base of his activities and his policy eventually proved to be so beneficial that his Company was firmly established on what has been demonstrated by time to be strong and viable foundations.

In the early post-war years, therefore, Henry Tyrer and Company successfully diversified in many ways. The formation of Freight Conveyors Limited, the extension of bunkering facilities, the agencies for the Southern Whaling and Sealing Company, Coast Lines and the British and Irish Steam Packet Company were all valuable additions to the firm's activities. Tyrer also strengthened his Company's position by extending its coastal service to southern Scotland, by improving the efficiency of its Liverpool and Preston offices and by maintaining its position in its traditional West African agency business. Then, at a later date, Henry Tyrer was able to interest the African and Eastern Trade Corporation in the possibility of carrying their own cargoes and eventually, by making the most of the difficulties between the newly established UAC and the Conference Lines, was successful in obtaining an important and profitable share in the West African shipping trade.

This is not to suggest that Henry Tyrer was in any way infallible for this would be far from the truth. He was, in fact, a shrewd entrepreneur who had made his way in a highly competitive trade by dint of his enthusiasm and ability to work very hard over long periods. His upbringing tended to make him over-cautious, perhaps even parsimonious in some respects — one of his favourite sayings was — 'Look after the pennies and the pounds will look after themselves.'[77]

This philosophy pervaded the Company and throughout his lifetime costs were kept to a very low level. Sometimes, however, this policy may have been taken to extremes so that efficiency was impaired, not enhanced, by the desire to save on expenditure. Thus the reluctance to use taxi-cabs for anything except the gravest emergencies resulted in a minor saving to the firm's petty cash and a major loss of man-power while documents and messages were relayed on foot. If Tyrer himself required a taxi the boy sent to secure it was under instructions to walk back — the meter could not then be set until the car reached the firm's office.[78]

In spite of this tendency Henry Tyrer had another side to his character and, on occasion, was careless and guilty of gross errors of judgement. The mistakes of 1890 when he over-reached himself to such an extent that he was only able to avoid bankruptcy by a whisker[79] were not repeated but he did make an unwise investment in the shares of the Port of Chicoutimi Limited, and was seriously tempted to invest in 'The Non-Collapsible Tyre Syndicate Limited'.[80] It was only a difficulty over patent rights which saved him on this latter occasion and, later, during the early post-war period it is again clear that not all of his decisions were based on sound economic analysis. Some indeed, show a distinct lack of awareness and suggest that he would sometimes act on impulse or perhaps from a desire to impress his business associates. Tyrer's Coasters, Limited,[81] would appear to be a case of this type and the immediate heavy losses which followed the opening of a London Office in 1922[82] indicates that the venture was insufficiently researched. There may, of course, be satisfactory explanations for these decisions and it could, at least, be argued that they were the consequences of a policy of expansion and diversification which, overall, was undoubtedly highly successful. There can be no such quibbles over Tyrer's disastrous approval of his Company's complicity in what became known as the 'Vestfos' affair.

The s.s. *Vestfos* of the Thor Thoresen Line of Oslo was loaded with woodpulp in Norway during July 1923. The cargo was consigned to Messrs Becker and Company at Preston who used the bills of lading to obtain an advance of £3,211 from the National Provincial Bank.[83] If normal commercial procedure had then been followed Becker's would have needed to redeem the bills of lading in order to obtain delivery of their goods from the ship. In fact, Tyrer's agreed to accept an indemnity under which Becker's merely guaranteed to produce the relevant documents at a later date. It subsequently transpired that this was a fairly common practice between Tyrer's and Becker's but on this occasion the bills of lading never materialised as the latter went bankrupt in October of that year.

The Thor Thoresens Line was then threatened with legal action by the Bank and eventually settled the matter by paying the sum of £2,500. Thoresens, in turn, threatened Henry Tyrer and Company and in the absence of any agreement the case came before the King's Bench Division in November 1929.[84] Tyrer's admitted that they had released the cargo without the bills of lading but argued that the Bank had acquiesced in this and previous arrangements. This was not disputed but Mr Justice Wright ruled that this in no way reduced Tyrer's responsibility and the Company was ordered to re-pay the £2,500 together with the full costs of the action.[85]

At the time of this incident and of similar errors of judgement (1919-23) Henry Tyrer was still running the Company on a personal basis and must take full responsibility for what were both irresponsible and illegal actions. The reasons for his attitude are made quite clear in the evidence provided by a member of the staff during the court hearing —

Mr Herbert Metcalf Warlow, manager at Preston for the defendants, gave evidence about previous cargoes which were released on indemnities given by the importers, Messrs Becker and Co. Ltd. He said that this was done because at that time (1923) Messrs Becker were of a very high financial standing and a very strong firm. Had the defendants refused to accept the indemnity there was grave danger that Messrs Becker would have withdrawn their shipping altogether from the plaintiff's line, for which the defendants might have been blamed. The defendants did not give anyone else the facilities they gave to Messrs Becker.[86]

It would seem, therefore, that Tyrer deliberately chose to engage in what he must have known was a 'risky' practice because of his desire to retain Becker's business. This was, as has already been noted, an important aspect of his activities but not so vital, in retrospect, to have justified a policy which went against every rule and tradition of agency work. Perhaps the uncertainties of the post-war slump led Tyrer to fear for the future of his Company — if so it suggests that the image of a hard, if fair, taskmaster which he usually adopted and seems to have encouraged, really concealed a human being with strengths and weaknesses like other ordinary mortals.

Henry Tyrer also had a generous streak in his make-up and was anxious that both his directors and staff should share in his firm's prosperity. Salaries, consequently, were reviewed annually and rises were granted to those individuals who appeared to deserve them, while general increases were made when changes in the cost of living made this essential. Few employees seemed to have been dissatisfied with pay and conditions and the turnover of staff was low. In fact the members of his Preston office thought so highly of him that in 1908 they presented him with a silver rose bowl to mark the occasion of his fiftieth birthday.[87] Henry Tyrer always adopted the policy of recruiting employees from his home district in the belief that they were less likely to cause difficulties than the 'city slickers' of Liverpool. Whether this view was correct is open to question — at a time of high unemployment it was unlikely that any sensible person would lightly leave a secure, if moderately paid, position. Tyrer undoubtedly operated in what, today, would be regarded as an autocratic manner but he did appear to have the welfare of his staff at heart. Thus while he insisted on devoted service he believed in incentives and organised a bonus system that rewarded hard work. While not a pace-setter in this field he also agreed to the establishment of a comprehensive pension scheme as early as 1930[88] but this still had not come into effect by the time of his death.[89]

Henry Tyrer's relationships with his fellow directors was more complex. Until the 1920s he took all the real decisions and the older employees who had become directors when the 'Limited' company was formed in 1914 might better be described as 'Departmental Managers'. These, too, were expected to work hard but, in turn, reaped fairly substantial returns. Their shareholdings were gradually increased although up to the time of his death Henry Tyrer continued to hold the vast majority of his firm's shares. The salaries of the directors showed much greater progress particularly when the Company was prosperous but even when business was poor Tyrer ensured that his senior colleagues did not suffer. In 1926, for example, Tyrer reduced his own drawings by £400 (from £1,650 to £1,250) in order to give Messrs Cutts, Stretch, Warlow and Wilson an extra £100 each.[90]

VII

From 1928 onwards Henry Tyrer's health began to fail and in that year he missed the Annual General Meeting for the first time.[91] Thereafter his attendance was somewhat irregular and he slowly took a less and less active part in the running of the business. In these circumstances his nephew, Mr Thomas Wilson, and Mr Frederick Cutts were given increasing authority and emerged as the new leaders of the enterprise. At first they moved very cautiously and Henry Tyrer was consulted on all matters of policy and administration but in the course of time only matters of substantial importance were referred to him.

Henry Tyrer's original illness was an attack of shingles. This left him in a weakened state and this was made worse by the death in 1929 of Mr H.E. Drain who had been an employee and, later, a director of his firm for forty years.[92] In spite of these difficulties Tyrer (together with Thomas Wilson) was able to play a significant part in persuading the UAC to carry their own cargoes[93] but from then onward his role within the Company was a much more passive one. He retained his room in the office at Royal Liver Building and acquired a new one when the firm moved to fresh premises at Africa House in 1933[94] but he came in less and less and spent more time at home, particularly with his garden. Tyrer was unwell again during the latter part of 1930[95] but it was not until 1933 when he required a small operation that his health really deteriorated.[96] From then onward he was extremely frail and his visits to his office were increasingly rare. Nevertheless his fellow directors remained very much aware of the need to retain his approval and he continued to guide the Company by attending the two general meetings that were held each year.

The illness of 1933 appears to have convinced Henry Tyrer of the fact of his own mortality and that his life was coming to an end. Consequently he began to think very seriously about the future of his firm and a number of decisions were taken. Securities which Tyrer had held in his own name were transferred to the Company — these included War Loan stock together with Ordinary and Preference shares in Lever Brothers Limited, Freight Conveyors Limited, John S. Monks Limited, the *Dampskibsaktielskapet Bjorn* and the Port of Chicoutimi Limited.[97] It is clear that Tyrer was also concerned about the continuation of family control of his enterprise because a combination of circumstances had prevented his original plans from coming to fruition.

In the absence of children of his own Henry Tyrer had decided at a much earlier date that his nephews should work in the firm and eventually succeed him. Thus John Edmund Wilson and Thomas Wilson (the sons of Henry's sister, Ann) were employed from an early age and the former was granted power of attorney to act on Tyrer's behalf when still a very young man.[98] Unfortunately John was killed while acting as super-cargo on s.s. *Prestonian's* second voyage to West Africa in 1904[99] but his brother, Thomas, worked his way up in the firm and was made one of the original directors when the Company acquired 'limited' status in 1914.

The two sons of another of Henry Tyrer's sisters, Jane, also worked for the firm. These were James Edward Lyon (Senior) and Harold Cuthbert Lyon, and the former was so highly thought of that, like Thomas Wilson, he was made a director in 1914. The outbreak of war resulted in James who had been in the Territorial Army being concerned with the training of recruits at Ormskirk[100] but this gradually palled and he volunteered for overseas service. Sadly, he was killed in action by a German shell after only a brief period in France – long enough, however, to have made a memorable impact on the officers and men of his regiment.[101] His brother, Harold, was employed in the Preston office but although a conscientious and well-liked individual he was not promoted to become a director during Henry Tyrer's lifetime.

In the early 1930s, therefore, Henry Tyrer employed two nephews, Thomas Wilson and Harold Lyon, in his firm. Both of these men were married but neither had any children and it appeared improbable by that time that they would then have any. In these circumstances, Tyrer turned his attention to the younger generation and two new members of his family were recruited. The first of these was James Edward Lyon (Junior), the posthumous son of Sgt Lyon and he left Ormskirk Grammar School a year before his time in direct response to Henry Tyrer's request. The second was Charles Wilson Harrison, son of Maud – the daughter of Henry's sister, Ann[102] – and like James Lyon he, too, was withdrawn from Ormskirk Grammar School twelve months earlier than had been anticipated.

The two newcomers joined the Company in mid 1933 and January, 1935, respectively. Both were obviously marked for promotion and possible eventual control but only if they could measure up to the high standards demanded by Henry Tyrer and whoever he nominated as his successors. The two boys each made a favourable impression on the Governing Director although by then he was spending very little time in his office. Apart from meeting him at business Lyon and Harrison also met Henry Tyrer when, on special occasions, they and their families visited him at 'Bewcastle'. These tended to be very formal affairs which the boys and their mothers regarded with some apprehension for, while Tyrer believed in maintaining his family connections, he had no time for frequent social gatherings.

James Lyon and Charles Harrison also attended 'Bewcastle' when in June 1935, Henry and Jane Elizabeth Tyrer reached their fiftieth wedding anniversary. The whole of the staff of the Liverpool and Preston offices were invited, together with employees from Manor House Farm, so that a total of more than sixty guests toasted the health of their hosts.[103] The two young clerks had little further chance to get to know Henry Tyrer for, by then, he was getting progressively weaker and seldom left his home. Nevertheless, Henry Tyrer continued to play some part in the running of the Company which bore his name and he was able to attend a meeting of directors which was held at Africa House on 30 December 1935.[104] His final attendance was at the Annual General Meeting of Freight Conveyors Limited which took place in Liverpool on 21 January 1936. Thereafter his influence was exercised through Thomas Wilson and Frederick Cutts who frequently called at 'Bewcastle' so as to consult him on various aspects of policy and tactics.

As the year progressed these meetings gradually changed their character and the business aspect became less and less important. Instead Henry Tyrer was more anxious to discuss other matters such as his home or garden: sometimes he merely encouraged his visitors to take him for a car trip round the neighbourhood. Everything pointed, in fact, to a steady physical decline so it came as no great surprise when he died after a brief attack of bronchitis on 20 June 1936.[105] Henry's widow, Jane Elizabeth Tyrer, then appeared to lose the will to live and she only survived him by two months —

> The loss of her husband, after 51 years of happy married life was a severe blow to Mrs Tyrer and one from which she had not been able to recover. Although not actually ill in a physical sense, she was in a somewhat enfeebled state of health, and was much affected by her great grief, but she had borne up courageously and endeavoured to display her usual bright spirit. On the day previous to her death she had been out visiting friends, but at one o'clock on Tuesday morning

her end came, suddenly, but peacefully.[106]

Henry had been in his 79th year and Jane Elizabeth had been in her 82nd year when they died. Both were buried in Rufford Parish Church in the same grave as their two infant children.[107]

Notes

1. Henry Tyrer MSS, *Director's Minute Book,* no. 1, 25 November 1918, p. 40.

2. Ibid., 25 November 1918, p. 39.

3. Ibid., 16 July 1920, p. 52.

4. See Appendix, Table 6, p. 142.

5. Henry Tyrer MSS, Box 2, letter from Canadian Pacific to Henry Tyrer, 4 February 1918.

6. Ibid., *Director's Minute Book,* no. 1, 1 October 1918, p. 38.

7. Ibid., 16 July 1920, p. 53.

8. Ibid., Box 46, Articles of Association of Freight Conveyors Limited.

9. Mr J.K. Greenhalgh was financial adviser to Lord Leverhulme at this time.

10. Public Records Office, Kew, file 165195: BT31 − 25695.

11. Ibid.

12. Heywood's MSS, Manager's Minute Book, 28 November 1919 and 23 March 1921, 11a.

13. This was the Richie Concrete Shipbuilding and Engineering Co Ltd.

14. Henry Tyrer MSS, Box 37, interview with Mr D. Ollerton.

15. Public Records Office, Kew, file 165195: BT31 − 25695.

16. Heywood's MSS, Manager's Minute Book, 18 March 1920, 11a.

17. Ibid.

18. I am indebted to Dr Gordon Jackson of Strathclyde University for this information. See G. Jackson, *The British Whaling Trade,* (A. & C. Black, London, 1978).

19. Henry Tyrer MSS, Box 22, Agreement dated 26 March 1921.

20. Ibid., letters from N. Charles Watt, Vice-Chairman of the Southern Whaling & Sealing Co Ltd, dated 25 January 1924 and 31 May 1929.

21. See above, Chapter 5, pp. 76-7.

22. Ibid., pp. 64-5.

23. Public Record Office, Kew, file 68156: BT31 − 16538.

24. Ibid., file 71816: BT − 18482.

25. Tyrer's were also to suffer a major loss when, following a delayed court action, they were forced to pay damages in respect of a cargo released to Becker and Company without proper documentation. See below, pp. 92-3.

26. Henry Tyrer MSS, *Director's Minute Book,* no. 1, 14 July 1924, p. 77.

27. Ibid.

28. Tyrer's owned 790 £1 Preference Shares in Becker & Co in 1922. Then, after the amalgamation with the Preston S.N. Co their holdings were converted into 4,130 Ordinary £1 shares. In 1924, when Becker was re-organised, Tyrer's possessed 4,920 Ordinary Shares. (See file 71816, at the Public Record Office, Kew).

29. Henry Tyrer MSS, *Director's Minute Book,* no. 1, 12 August 1922, p. 64.

30. Ibid.

31. Ibid., 3 August 1923, p. 65.

32. Ibid., 12 May 1924, p. 74.

33. Ibid., 14 July 1924, p. 78.

34. Henry Tyrer MSS, Box 19, Agreement between Henry Tyrer & Co Ltd and Coast Lines Ltd and the British & Irish S.P. Co Ltd dated 26 June 1924.

35. Ibid.

36. Ibid., letter from James W. Ratledge, Director of Coast Lines Ltd, to Henry Tyrer & Co Ltd, dated 18 October 1928.

37. This was later changed to S.E. Collingwood Dock.

38. Henry Tyrer MSS, Box 37, interview with Mr D. Ollerton.

39. Ibid., *Director's Minute Book*, no. 1, 29 December 1924, p. 79.

40. Ibid., Box 37, interview with Mr D. Ollerton.

41. Ibid., Box 18, correspondence with Stockwood, Rees & Co Ltd.

42. The 'Camel' brand of liquors and spirits had been registered by H.B.W. Russell and Company in Nigeria in 1905 in spite of the claim made by the Netherlands Distilleries of Schiedam that this brand had been used by them for many years. The two firms had reached an agreement in 1913 whereby the Netherlands Distilleries continued to use the 'Camel' trade mark but paid Russell's a small commission. This arrangement had come to an end during the war but Tyrer's were eventually able to suggest a compromise so that the commission was restored at 1½d per case: the Netherlands Distilleries then obtained legal title to the brand but, in turn, transferred their 'The Three Legs' and 'Serpent' marks to Russell's. (See: Henry Tyrer MSS, Box 36, correspondence with Netherlands Distilleries and H.B.W. Russell & Co Ltd, and Agreement between these firms dated 5 November 1925.)

43. Henry Tyrer MSS, *Director's Minute Book,* no. 1, 24 November 1925, p. 90.

44. Ibid., 10 July 1925, p. 82.

45. Ibid., 17 July 1925, p. 86.

46. Ibid., 17 July 1925, p. 84.

47. Ibid., 17 February 1925, p. 81.

48. Henry Tyrer MSS, Box 17. Tyrer's never found it necessary to utilise this site and it was sold with considerable profit in 1959.

49. *The History of the United Africa Co Ltd to 1938,* published privately by the Company (London, 1938), p. 93.

50. P.N. Davies, *The Trade Makers, Elder Dempster in West Africa, 1852-1972* (George Allen and Unwin, London, 1972), p. 212.

51. Ibid., p. 224.

52. Heywood's MSS, Manager's Minute Book, no. 12, 5 October 1923, p. 159.

53. Henry Tyrer MSS, Box 3.

54. Ibid.

55. *Woodville* had previously been owned by the Southern Whaling and Sealing Company and had had the distinction of carrying the body of Sir Ernest Shackleton for burial in South Georgia.

56. Henry Tyrer MSS, Box 3.

57. In fact, the Conference Lines gave the Niger Company a bigger discount than the African and Eastern and this came to light when the two firms amalgamated to form the United Africa Company in 1929. See Davies, *The Trade Makers,* pp. 262-3.

58. Henry Tyrer MSS, Box 5, voyage 6.

59. Ibid., voyage 4.

60. *Ars,* of 2,936 gross tons, had been built in 1897 so was thirty-one years old when she was acquired. See Captain G.G. Astbury, DSC 'The Master Remembers', in *Palm Bulletin,* vol. V, no. II (1964), pp. 16-18 and no. III (1964), pp. 13-15.

61. See above, p. 86.

62. F. Pedler, *The Lion and the Unicorn in Africa: A History of the Origins of the United Africa Company, 1787-1931* (Heinemann, London, 1974), pp. 297-8.

63. *Who Was Who,* 1951-1960, p. 226.

64. Davies, *The Trade Makers,* p. 238.

65. Ibid., pp. 239-44.

66. Henry Tyrer MSS, Box 6.

67. Ibid., Box 32, interview with Mr R.L. Jones who was in the office with Mr T. Wilson when the telegram arrived.

68. See above, pp. 87-8.

69. These were formerly *Laurel Branch* and *Cambrian Empress* and had been built in 1903 and 1907 respectively.

70. Author's interview with Mr Donald E. Erlebach in March 1966.

71. Henry Tyrer MSS, Box 6, UAC MSS.

72. Davies, *The Trade Makers,* p. 283.

73. C. Wilson, *The History of Unilever* (Cassell, London, 1954), pp. 370-2.

74. Davies, *The Trade Makers,* p. 284.

75. See Appendix 7, p. 144 for details of the growth of trade with Nigeria and the Gold Coast.

76. See the *Annual Reports of the Chamber of Shipping of the UK* for the relevant years.

77. Henry Tyrer MSS, Box 32, interview with Mr R.L. Jones

78. Author's interview with Mr J.E. Lyon, June 1978.

79. See above, Chapter 2, pp. 31-3.

80. Henry Tyrer MSS, Box 45, correspondence with the Non-Collapsible Tyre Syndicate Ltd, and with Mr H.J. Mouritz during April, 1901.

81. See above, p. 81.

82. See above, p. 84.

83. *Lloyd's List Law Reports,* H.P. Henley (ed), Michaelmas Sittings, 1929, vol. 35, p. 163.

84. The hearing was delayed by the lengthy task of liquidating and re-organising Becker and Company.

85. The total cost to Tyrer's amounted to £3,818: See *Director's Minute Book,* no. 1, 1 July 1930, p. 123.

86. *Lloyd's List Law Reports,* p. 164.

87. This is now in the possession of Mr J.E. Lyon.

88. *Director's Minute Book,* no. 1, 1 July 1930, p. 126.

89. Ibid., 3 July 1935, p. 157.

90. Ibid., 26 July 1926, p. 94.

91. Ibid., 26 June 1928, p. 107.

92. Ibid., 21 December 1929, p. 117.

93. See above, p. 89.

94. *Director's Minute Book,* no. 1, 1 January 1933, p. 140.

95. Ibid., 23 December 1930, p. 128.

96. Ibid., 22 December 1933, p. 146.

97. Ibid., 7 February 1934, p. 148.

98. Henry Tyrer MSS, Box 30, Power of Attorney, dated 22 June 1900.

99. See above, Chapter 3, p. 46.

100. Henry Tyrer MSS, Box 37, interview with Mr D. Ollerton.

101. Ibid., Box 40, letter from Commanding Officer, 'A' Company, 1/9th KLR, to Mrs Lyon, 26 August 1917. See Appendix, Table 8, p. 145.

102. See Appendix, Table 1, p. 137, for details of Henry Tyrer's family tree.

103. *Ormskirk Advertiser,* 'A Lathom Golden Wedding', 20 June 1935.

104. Henry Tyrer MSS, *Director's Minute Book,* no. 1, 30 December 1935,

p. 160.
105. *Ormskirk Advertiser,* 'Death of Mr Henry Tyrer . . .', 25 June 1936.
106. Ibid., 'Sudden Death of Mrs H. Tyrer', 27 August 1936.
107. See above, Chapter 2, p. 28.

7 THE SECOND WORLD WAR

I

The death of Henry Tyrer was not unexpected as for several years his health had been gradually deteriorating. As a direct consequence his attendance at his office had declined so that in his last year he only came in occasionally for a few hours. In these circumstances the direction of Henry Tyrer and Company had fallen increasingly upon Thomas Wilson (Henry's nephew) and on Frederick Cutts who had joined the firm in 1897. In his latter days Henry Tyrer seems to have relied upon them for support in equal measure and apparently held both in high esteem. Nevertheless when he set about apportioning his estate he clearly felt that 'blood was thicker than water' and so he instructed that Thomas Wilson should follow him as head of the firm.

Henry Tyrer's will directed that a number of bequests should be settled as soon as possible after his death and that the balance of his estate should then be held in trust for his wife. The fact that Jane Elizabeth Tyrer died very quickly after her husband meant in practice that the will was dealt with as a whole and that many of its provisions were nullified. Tyrer left just over £50,000 (gross) and after all obligations and instructions had been met a net sum of £24,075 remained.[1] This was then divided amongst the 'residuary legatees' — Tyrer's nephews, nieces, great niece and great nephew — who each received £1,715. In addition, each was left £187 of War Loan stock which, like the shares in Henry Tyrer & Company Limited, were specifically allocated under the terms of the will.[2]

At the time of his death Henry Tyrer owned 1,500 Preference and 12,436 Ordinary shares in his Company. According to his instructions the vast majority of the latter were left to his two nephews, Mr Thomas Wilson and Mr Harold Cuthbert Lyon, who both received 5,843 shares each.[3] This gave them full control of the firm so while Mr Wilson succeeded Henry Tyrer as Governing Director, Mr Lyon became a Director for the first time.

Thomas Wilson, son of Ann Wilson the sister of Henry Tyrer, had joined his uncle's firm as a boy and had become one of its original directors when it achieved 'limited' status in 1914.[4] During Tyrer's declining years Wilson and Frederick Cutts had effectively run the Company and this arrangement continued after his death. They appeared to get on well together but they were entirely different personalities. Thus while Mr Cutts tended to overawe people, Mr Wilson had a warmer character and although he could be sharp when mistakes were made he quickly ended any disagreements and never bore a grudge. His inclination was always to try to keep things on the go even if this sometimes meant cutting a few corners: 'While we've got our ships moving we're making money, you see.'[5] On the other hand Mr Cutts tended to be more cautious so together the two senior directors formed a balanced team which was quite capable of continuing the policies laid down by Henry Tyrer.

At first the new Governing Director seemed happy to follow in Henry Tyrer's footsteps and sought only to maintain the firm's traditional interests as efficiently as possible. As time went on, however, and he 'found his feet' he gradually introduced various changes. One of the first of these was the re-organisation of Freight Conveyors Limited which, as noted earlier,[6] had been established in 1919 to undertake Tyrer's stevedoring in the port of Liverpool. This had been achieved with the aid of three members of the Greenhalgh family but Samuel had died in 1930 and Harry Jimpson had ceased to be the Managing Director in 1932. Thus when Henry Tyrer died in 1936 H.J. Greenhalgh was an ordinary director and his cousin, J.K. Greenhalgh, was the company's auditor. Both had been associated with Freight Conveyors from its inception but in view of Tyrer's death and of their advancing years the new controllers of Henry Tyrer and Company Limited, decided to make a fresh start. Accordingly the original firm, Freight Conveyors Limited, was wound up voluntarily in 1937[7] and a new concern, Freight Conveyors (1937) Limited, was formed to continue with its work.[8]

Thomas Wilson also encouraged the development of the road haulage links which had originally been inaugurated by Henry Tyrer in the mid-1920s. At that time Tyrer's had been the Merseyside Agents for Tyne Ferries, White Star Transport and Liveseys Motors and frequently arranged return loads from Liverpool docks. This involvement sometimes provided small loads, usually of a multi-destination character, for which it was difficult to find haulage. Henry Tyrer used this knowledge to aid a number of Ormskirk men to find employment. He did this by providing them with loans for the purchase of suitable vehicles and then arranged for them to carry the loads not wanted by the bigger firms. Jack Oldfield, Charles Fardoe and Henry Caunce were three who benefited in this way during Tyrer's lifetime when the whole business was of relatively small importance.[9] Thomas Wilson, however, saw this as a useful method of diversification and the Transport Department showed healthy gains in each year before the onset of the Second World War.[10]

Thomas Wilson had always been on the West African side of the business and he continued to act as the main link with the United Africa Company even after he had succeeded Henry Tyrer as the Head of the firm. As Governing Director, however, he also concerned himself with other aspects of the firm's activities and it was due to his initiative that Tyrer's were appointed as Liverpool Agents for the Norwegian America Line Inc. of Oslo.[11] This line operated between Norway and the United States and for a while provided a small but valuable extension to Tyrer's agency business by operating a service between America and Liverpool. Unfortunately this development, like many others, came to an abrupt end with the commencement of hostilities in September 1939, but Tyrer's found that war-time dislocation brought many Norwegian American ships into the ports so the agency continued to provide useful additional business.

II

The three years between the death of Henry Tyrer and the beginning of the Second World War saw a slight decline from the very high levels of profit achieved in the period from 1933 to 1936. Nevertheless it proved quite possible to maintain the ordinary share dividend at 20% — a return only previously achieved on exceptional occasions — so it will be appreciated that Thomas Wilson had been extremely successful in maintaining the Company's position.

Thus in the seventeen month period which ended on 30 September 1938,[12] Tyrer's made a net profit of £7,567 at Liverpool which together with £882 from Preston meant a total of £8,450.[13] During this time Liverpool had dealt with 314 deep-sea and 383 coastal vessels, while Preston had acted for 206 foreign, 93 coastal and 64 cattle ships.[14] The major principal at Liverpool was the United Africa Company for whom 48 ships were handled (5 others were turned round for the Southern Whaling and Sealing Company) while at Preston the cattle trade operated for Coast Lines was clearly of the greatest importance, although the links with Scandinavia were also quite significant.[15]

A period of dislocation and re-adjustment followed the out-break of war and Tyrer's found themselves to be only lightly employed. This was mainly due to the re-routing of vessels and the introduction of the convoy system and it was expected that as trade settled down into fresh avenues the level of activity would gradually return to normal. There is some evidence that this was happening but the escalation of the conflict to include Norway and Denmark had a disastrous effect on the trade at Preston and the Company found it necessary to review its financial affairs. The position was then regarded as being so serious that at a meeting held on 23 April 1940, it was decided that it was not possible to raise their employees wages even though other firms were doing so and that the salaries of the directors must be cut by 25% at once.[16]

Paradoxically business began to improve almost immediately and although many of Tyrer's traditional interests remained depressed, work for the Ministry of War Transport more than offset these losses. Thus while services to Scandinavia and the Continent came to an end and restrictions on whaling led to Lever's selling the Southern Whaling and Sealing Company,[17] the coastal, Irish and West African trades all recovered to a satisfactory extent. In addition, Tyrer's were appointed as agents for the army in Northern Ireland so were responsible for shipping huge quantities of supplies from Preston to Belfast.[18] It was the work for the Ministry, however, which really ensured that Tyrer's were kept at full stretch from 1940 to the end of the war in 1945.

At Liverpool the Ministry of War Transport nominated a Port Director and he was placed in control of the whole of the docks. All stevedoring was then 'pooled' and Freight Conveyors were allocated certain sections which they operated irrespective of the vessels which arrived. In practice, however, they were mainly ships belonging to Alfred Holt and Elder Dempster but others were dealt with as necessary and, at times, the staff were obliged to work night and day —

... and of course at that time I was working from 18 to 20 hours a day, and we were working nights. We would go home and have a bite to eat and come back (to the docks) by 11 o'clock and see the ship started and stay till about midnight, go home, have a sleep and come back early the next morning.[19]

Wartime dislocation meant that some vessels which formerly visited Liverpool and Preston were diverted to different ports. The other side of this picture was that ships which did not normally come to these ports might now suddenly appear. Thus Agency Agreements which in peacetime had resulted in only small amounts of business for Tyrer's might overnight mean a great deal of extra work.[20] In addition, when ships came in whose owners were not represented at the port the Ministry would frequently make an arbitrary decision as to who should handle her and Tyrer's received their full share of vessels of this type.

Amongst the many ships handled by Tyrer's at Liverpool during this period were two 'Merchant Aircraft Carriers', the *Empire MacAlpine* and the *Empire MacKendrick*. These were both managed by William Thomson and Company of Edinburgh who also managed the Ben Line and it was partly as a result of this connection that Tyrer's were appointed as agents for the Ben Line at Liverpool.[21] This was an event which, as will be seen later,[22] was to have vital consequences in the post-war era.

At Preston the workload became equally heavy once the initial difficulties had been overcome and it became necessary to arrange for special overdraft facilities as Tyrer's paid out for 'coasters commandeered by Government, and paid out for Hospital Ship in Preston Dock. The Ministry are slow to repay these expenses.'[23]

By May 1941, the Preston Office was very busy indeed for as well as the rapidly growing trade with Northern Ireland and Eire, large numbers of unscheduled vessels were increasingly using the port '. . . 3 or 4 ships may call at once and each may require up to £900 for expenses, pay etc. The staff are working till 8 pm at night, seven days per week. Ninety ships have been dealt with during the last three months.'[24]

The financial results of all these activities were to prove extremely satisfactory. Tyrer's disappointments during the early days of the war were replaced by returns which proved to be the highest in the firm's history. Thus the gross profit for 1939 was only £2,699, but for 1940 it was £8,265; 1941 amounted to £7,630; 1942 (£8,614); 1943 (£12,128); 1944 (£10,414) and 1945 (£8,010).[25] These figures allowed a 20% dividend to be paid on the ordinary shares during 1943 and 1944 while a 30% dividend was paid in 1945. At the same time the Company's reserves were also built up quite substantially so Tyrer's ended the war in a very strong position.[26]

It should be remembered that these results were achieved at a time of great difficulty. At least eighteen members of staff joined the armed services and a number of others were 'seconded' for work of national importance.[27] Thus Mr J. Norris, one of Tyrer's most experienced employees, was transferred to assist the Ministry of War Transport's administration.[28] As a consequence there was always a shortage of senior people and the older employees were obliged to do more than their fair share. Much of Tyrer's work was also undertaken when the danger from enemy bombing was very real and, even after this was over, the physical disruption had to be overcome by special arrangements which involved even more work for the hard pressed staff.

Tyrer's certainly appreciated the efforts made by their employees during this period and every effort was made to ease their burdens. Bonuses and increases in wages became a regular feature of the director's annual reports and when any employee was conscripted the Company agreed to pay them the difference between their normal salary and that received from HM Forces.[29] The real reward to the more senior staff came, however, in 1942 when Sydney Dalzell, John Merriweather, James Campbell McNeill, Dick Ollerton, John Pilkington and George Sanders were all appointed as directors of the Company. At the same time it was agreed that Thomas Wilson, Frederick Cutts and Mr H.M. Warlow be elected as managing directors.[30] This was a sensible arrangement for it recognised that Tyrer's were operating in three distinct spheres of activity and formalised the management structure so that Mr Warlow looked after the Preston office, Mr Cutts saw to the agency business at Liverpool and Mr Wilson, while retaining an overall control of the Company, was responsible for the organisation of the West African trade.

III

When the newly formed United Africa Company (UAC) failed to reach agreement with the West African Lines Conference in 1929, Henry Tyrer and Company were asked to make the necessary arrangements for the carriage of its cargoes. At first this required the services of many chartered vessels[31] but gradually, and for a variety of reasons, the size of the fleet owned by the UAC began to increase.[32] This build up meant additional employment for Tyrer's though, of course, they chartered on a much more limited scale.[33] By the outbreak of war, therefore, most of the UAC's requirements were being met by Company owned tonnage and this activity constituted a major part of Tyrer's work. The system changed dramatically in September 1939, for the ending of the sailings of the (German) Woermann Line and of the Holland West Africa Line meant that insufficient tonnage was available for what was regarded as an essential trade. Accordingly the Government gave instructions for the formation of a West African Co-ordination Committee and this included representatives of Elder Dempster, John Holt and of the United Africa Company.[34]

The new body then acted on behalf of the Ministry of War Transport as the regulating authority for the West African trade. In practice it organised the booking of all outward cargoes, utilising the facilities of the three participants on a joint basis. In the course of time homeward freight also came under the auspices of various United Kingdom ministries and the allocation of shipping space for all voyages became virtually complete. In these circumstances commercial considerations rapidly gave way to the national interest and because of the policy of retaining firms on the routes where they had special knowledge and experience the system proved to be highly satisfactory.

The withdrawal of the German and Dutch lines, together with the requisitioning of many vessels for specific wartime purposes meant that shipping space was always in short supply. This was alleviated to some extent by the transfer of vessels from non-operative or less important services but, in turn, these were offset by the ever-growing demands for West African products. Thus it was essential that each ship be packed to the limit of her capacity and that turn round be achieved as quickly as possible. These objectives were largely obtained by the dedication of the organising staff of which Henry Tyrer employees formed an important part and their efforts became even more vital as enemy action against West African shipping routes began to take its toll.

Elder Dempster, the most important operator, lost half of its pre-war fleet of 228,777 gross tons during the period of hostilities[35] while John Holt lost three of their five peacetime ships plus one wartime replacement.[36] The Shipping Department of the United Africa Company also suffered grievous losses so that nine of the sixteen vessels owned in 1939 were sunk. Thus,

> ... *Congonian* was torpedoed off Freetown and *Kumasian* off the West Coast of Ireland. *Lafian* and *Zarian,* the latter having survived an earlier torpedoing, were sunk off the Azores whilst *Nigerian* met her fate south east of Trinidad. *Lagosian,* which on an earlier occasion had been bombed and set on fire, was sunk off Rio de Oro. *Matadian* was torpedoed at the entrance to the River Niger, *Dahomian* close to Cape Town and *Ashantian* in mid-Atlantic. The fleet was further depleted by the seizure of two vessels — *Gambian* and *Takoradian* — which were held in Dakar by Vichy France, whilst two others — *Guinean* and *Leonian* — served under the White Ensign for the duration of the war and were, in fact, the only two ships in the fleet to escape unscathed.[37]

It was possible, fortunately, to have three new vessels built during 1942 and 1943 but even with their support the fleet was clearly inadequate to meet the demands made upon it. Tyrer's, under the personal direction of Thomas Wilson, played a vital role in ensuring that the tonnage which still remained to the UAC was employed as efficiently as possible. The long association between Tyrer's and the UAC bore handsome fruit in this period for it was only the experience and understanding of the key men on both sides that enabled the many shortages and physical difficulties to be overcome. The introduction of additional

ships which were managed for the Ministry of War Transport then provided the means by which the cargoes could be moved on something
like the desired scale but these would have been of little value without
the determination of those concerned to make the most careful use of
what was available. This co-operation, and the spirit which underlay it,
was to prove invaluable in ensuring that Tyrer's retained the UAC agency
for a significant period after the war had come to an end.

IV

The defeat of Germany in 1945 saw Henry Tyrer and Company in a
strong financial position. They were also held in high regard by their
principal client, the United Africa Company, and could reasonably
expect that in the course of time their other traditional interests would
gradually revive. This is not to suggest that it was thought that the firm
would automatically return to its former eminence in each of its chosen
trades. On the contrary, it was anticipated that the ending of the war
would see a sharpening of the commercial rivalry which had always
characterised the shipping business in Liverpool. It was felt, however,
that in addition to these problems the post-war era would offer great
opportunities and that as the younger members of the staff returned
from their wartime duties a balanced team would be created that would
ensure Tyrer's continued prosperity.

Basic to this conception of the future was the understanding that
Thomas Wilson and Frederick Cutts would remain together to lead the
Company. Unfortunately this was not to be for Thomas Wilson died of
a heart attack on 16 May 1945, and the 'partnership' which had done
so much to guide the firm through the difficult days of the war came to
a premature end.

Frederick Cutts was an obvious choice to succeed Thomas Wilson.
He had seen the Company grow from a tiny firm to a business that
dominated the port of Preston and played an important role on Merseyside. He was regarded by Henry Tyrer as his right-hand man and Thomas
Wilson thought so highly of him that at one Shareholders Meeting he
stated that, '. . . he did not know what we would do without him.'[38]

In spite of these accolades it was by no means certain that Mr Cutts
would be elected to be chairman and to continue as managing director.[39]
Unlike Henry Tyrer and Thomas Wilson, Frederick Cutts held only a
few shares in the Company and so was completely dependent upon
external support. At this time, in fact, his holding of ordinary shares
was a bare 951 out of a total of 18,442,[40] but in view of his long experience and in the absence of a serious challenger he naturally assumed the

position of acting chairman until such time as the matter could be decided by a meeting of shareholders.

A major factor in the selection of a new chairman was the age of Mr Cutts who was then 65. This was undoubtedly felt to be of considerable importance by the United Africa Company whose attitude was clearly expressed in a letter from its managing director, Mr Frank Samuel, in August 1945:

> It is hardly necessary for me to tell you that during the very many years that we have been closely associated with Tyrer's in connection with our ships, we have been completely happy and satisfied, but the fact remains that Mr Wilson's death and your own age will require that we study the position most closely in order to assure that our arrangements for the future will fully protect our interests.[41]

A meeting was then arranged between Mr Cutts and Mr Samuel during which the situation was fully discussed:

> ... I told you that it was of immense concern to us to assure that as a result of Mr Wilson's death there was no falling away in the efficiency of the management of our fleet. Both you and Mr Wilson had expressed your opinion that your three junior directors were thoroughly capable people in whom great confidence could be reposed as regards the future management of the organisation. I told you that I had no reason to doubt that judgement, but felt the matter was of such very great importance to us that we would not be justified in depending entirely upon it, and that our own judgement could only be formed after seeing these gentlemen at work shouldering greater responsibilities during the next few years.
>
> In order to protect our position, and additionally having regard to the fact that you yourself have reached the age of 65 and consequently must within a comparatively few years be contemplating retirement, we felt the need of introducing into the business a man in whom we had the fullest confidence and who would work as part of the Tyrer team. I told you that we had Captain Astbury in mind, and you reacted favourably to the idea which you regarded as a sound and desirable one.[42]

A number of other matters were also discussed and agreed. These were mainly designed to provide financial incentives for Tyrer's directors who — for the most part — possessed only a small share in the Company's equity capital. Significantly, perhaps, Samuel concluded his letter to Cutts outlining these arrangement by stating '. . . I did not refer to it specifically, but I am of course taking it for granted that you will be appointed Chairman of Henry Tyrer in Wilson's place.'[43]

Frederick Cutts and his fellow directors welcomed Captain Astbury[44] to the Board of Henry Tyrer's in April 1946, and thus the Company was able to retain the confidence – and the Agency – of the UAC. It also meant that the arrangements under which the UAC shared in the profits which accrued from the loading and unloading of their vessels could continue.

As noted earlier[45] Freight Conveyors Limited had been reconstructed in 1937 and became Freight Conveyors (1937) Limited. Part of the reason for this change was that Lever's felt that as Tyrer's subsidiary, Freight Conveyors, undertook all the stevedoring at Liverpool, Tyrer's automatically obtained an additional profit on every cargo they handled.

In return Tyrer's had suggested that if Freight Conveyors did not do the work then other firms would have to be employed and they would naturally expect to earn some reward for their efforts. This argument brought forward the response that the proposed 'other firm' might as well be a Lever company, but when it was appreciated that this was a business that required considerable expertise a compromise was eventually reached. Under this arrangement a wholly owned subsidiary of Lever Brothers – Liver Transport Limited[46] – was made responsible for the loading and unloading of all UAC ships at Liverpool. Both the UAC and Tyrer's nominated the directors of the firm and Freight Conveyors provided the administration. In practical terms Liver Transport and Freight Conveyors then worked as a single organisation but at the end of each financial year the profits were divided according to the amount of cargo which each had brought into the business. Mr R.L. Jones of Freight Conveyors acted as the first secretary of Liver Transport and was largely responsible for the joint-workings of the two companies.[47] When Thomas Wilson died in 1945, Mr Jones was made a director of both firms, and continued to direct them until the whole situation was changed in 1950.[48]

V

The first AGM of Tyrer's shareholders which was held after the death of Thomas Wilson duly accepted Frederick Cutts as its new chairman.[49] By then he had already come to terms with the United Africa Company so that its agency had been assured for the foreseeable future and the position of Freight Conveyors Limited had been protected, in so far as was possible, by the continuation of the arrangement with Liver Transport Limited. Thus Tyrer's major customer continued to provide a substantial amount of work and this was of great value in the uncertain days of the early post-war period when many of Tyrer's other trades were slow to re-start.

The ending of lease-lend led to a reduction in imports into Liverpool and the position was not helped by a five weeks dock strike.[50] At Preston the cross-channel trade to Belfast and Dublin remained good but some vessels had to be diverted to other ports because of the poor state of the river.[51] This was a consequence of the lack of constant dredging which sometimes resulted in a draught that was too shallow to permit the larger vessels to enter the port. This has been a continuing problem at Preston and has obviously contributed to the decline of what was once a very busy harbour. Gradually, however, these difficulties were either overcome or reduced and with the re-emergence of the Norwegian woodpulp trade and the growth of the coastal and Irish services the Company achieved increasingly handsome returns. Consequently, while only £6,683 gross profit was made in 1946, £9,128 followed in 1947, £12,688 in 1948 and £14,218 in 1949.[52]

This reasonably happy picture tended, unfortunately, to obscure a number of unwelcome developments. On a personal basis these included the death of Mr H.M. Warlow who died in May 1948, after having fifty years service with the Company[53] and of more general impact was the nationalisation of road transport which eventually led to the ending of the activities of Tyrer's transport department.[54] Of much more fundamental importance, however, were the changes which were taking place in the West African shipping trade.

The wartime co-operation between Elder Dempster and the Shipping Departments of John Holts and the United Africa Company had been extremely successful so had been continued throughout the early post-war years. This had enabled full use to be made of scarce tonnage so had been welcomed both by the Merchants Freight Association and by the West African Produce Control Board.[55] The latter, which had been created during the war, exerted a virtual monopoly over the export of West African products and so had brought about a significant change in the organisation of the trade. In pre-war days many import merchants were also export merchants but under the new system they merely acted as buying agents for the Board or its successors. This had obvious consequences for firms like John Holt's and the UAC who had built up fleets of vessels to carry their own cargoes in *both* directions. By maintaining the wartime system of co-operation Holts and the UAC were continuing to act as common carriers and thus obtained a share of the Northbound cargoes which were moved on behalf of the Marketing Boards. During a time of shipping shortage this situation was accepted by all but as the supply of vessels improved pressure developed for all produce to be carried by independent operators.[56]

In these circumstances John Holts and the UAC decided to re-organise their shipping interests so that they were divorced from their functions as merchants.[57] This policy then resulted in the formation of the John Holt Line Limited (later the Guinea Gulf Line) and of the Palm Line. Thereafter the two new shipping firms had no direct connection with their parent companies and after becoming full members of the West African Lines Conference in 1950 carried freight for all merchants and Boards without distinction.[58]

These changes led the Palm Line to believe that, 'the management of their shipping interests at the principal place of business, Liverpool, should be dealt with in their own name instead of ourselves as their agents . . .' [59]

It was further stated that,

> . . . a circular letter will be issued by the Palm Line explaining the reason for this change in order that the public will understand the reason and will not be under the impression that Tyrer's services have been dispensed with through negligence or inattention . . .[60]

The termination of the UAC agency was subsequently undertaken on most amicable terms and it was specifically arranged so that no members of Tyrer's staff suffered the loss of their employment. Clearly the ending of a significant and longstanding segment of Tyrer's business implied that the Company would be over-staffed for a considerable time to come. On the other hand, the decision to establish a separate office for the Palm Line would have necessitated the recruitment and training of a large number of specialised personnel. Consequently, the mutually beneficial policy was adopted whereby the whole of Tyrer's management and employees were split into two parts. The first group which included three directors (Captain Astbury, J.C. McNeill and John Merriweather) agreed to leave the Company to set up the new organisation for the Palm Line, whilst the remainder of the directors and staff stayed with Tyrer's whose other interests were sufficient to keep them fully employed.

The same spirit of co-operation governed the provision of new premises for the two companies. Palm were anxious to remain in what had

been Tyrer's office at Africa House so offered the sum of £2,000 to
assist the latter to convert and modify alternative accommodation.[61] A
suitable office was then secured at Pioneer Buildings in Dale Street and
on 13 May 1950, Henry Tyrer and Company Limited, entered their
new domain and began a fresh chapter of their long history.

Notes

1. In addition Henry Tyrer left 1,500 6% Preference Shares @ £1 and 12,436
Ordinary Shares in Henry Tyrer and Company Limited. The latter were valued at
£2. 6s 8d for taxation purposes so his total holding amounted to £30,475 (£28,975
plus £1,500). When this sum is added to his other assets it will be seen that the
gross value of the estate was nearly £81,000.
2. Henry Tyrer MSS, Box 26, Will of Henry Tyrer dated 22 March 1932, and
Summary of Estate to 31 December 1939.
3. Ibid.
4. He was born at Ormskirk on 19 October 1883.
5. Henry Tyrer MSS, Box 32, interview with Mr R.L. Jones.
6. See above, Chapter 6, p. 81.
7. Freight Conveyors Limited, *Director's Minute Book,* 22 January 1937,
p. 103.
8. Note that the UAC took this opportunity to introduce their own firm, Liver
Transport Limited, and that this subsequently shared in the stevedoring of their
own vessels. See below, p. 110 and Chapter 8, p. 115.
9. Henry Tyrer MSS, Box 48a, interview with Mr John Lea, 26 July 1978.
10. Ibid., *Director's Minute Book,* no. 1, pp. 167, 173 and 181.
11. Henry Tyrer MSS, Box 32, interview with Mr R.L. Jones, 26 July 1978.
12. The end of the financial year was moved at this time from 30 April to 30
September.
13. Henry Tyrer MSS, *Director's Minute Book,* no. 1, 23 November 1938,
p. 173.
14. Ibid.
15. Ibid.
16. Ibid., p. 179.
17. Henry Tyrer MSS, Box 22, the Southern Whaling and Sealing Company
was sold to Salvesens's of Leith in 1941.
18. Ibid., Box 33, interview with Mr N.C. Harris, 9 August 1977.
19. Ibid., Box 32, interview with Mr R.L. Jones, 14 July 1977.
20. Ibid.
21. Ibid., Box 49, note by Mr J.E. Lyon.
22. See below, Chapter 8, pp. 116, 118 and 126.
23. Henry Tyrer MSS, Box 31, reference to Tyrer's Account at the Midland
Bank, Preston, in January 1941.
24. Ibid., May 1941.
25. Henry Tyrer MSS, *Director's Minute Book,* no. 1, pp. 177, 181, 183, 188,
193, 196 and 202.
26. Ibid.
27. Henry Tyrer MSS, Box 5, Mr F. Cutts, Notebook 'B'.
28. Ibid., Box 37, interview with Mr D. Ollerton, 29 November 1977.
29. Ibid., Box 5, Mr F. Cutts, Notebook 'B'.
30. Henry Tyrer MSS, *Director's Minute Book,* no. 1, 19 February 1943,
p. 189.

31. See above, Chapter 6, p. 89.

32. Ibid., pp. 89-90.

33. Henry Tyrer MSS, *Director's Minute Book,* no. 1, 23 November 1938, p. 173.

34. Davies, *The Trade Makers,* pp. 294-6.

35. Ibid., p. 301.

36. P.N. Davies, *A Short History of the Ships of John Holt & Co (Liverpool) Ltd and the Guinea Gulf Line Ltd* (John Holt, Liverpool, 1965), published privately, p. 10.

37. Henry Tyrer MSS, Box 6.

38. Henry Tyrer MSS, *Director's Minute Book,* no. 1, 19 February 1943, p. 189.

39. The title of 'Governing Director' was discontinued at this time.

40. Henry Tyrer MSS, Box 5, Mr F. Cutts, Notebook 'B'.

41. Ibid., Box 6, letter from F. Samuel to F. Cutts, 20 August 1945.

42. Ibid., 30 August 1945.

43. Ibid.

44. Captain G.G. Astbury, DSC, had been the first master of *Ars* when she was bought by the Niger Company in 1928 and had spent the remainder of his career with the Shipping Department of the UAC; see: Captain G.G. Astbury, DSC, 'The Master Remembers' in *Palm Bulletin,* vol. V, no. II (1964), pp. 16-18 and no. III (1964), pp. 13-15.

45. See above, p. 102.

46. Liver Transport Limited (Registration no. 314665) was formed in 1936 and began operations in 1937. Its name was changed to A.J. Seward & Co Ltd in 1961 when its objectives were changed to include work with chemicals and chandlery. Egwanga Ltd (Registration no. 86971) was formed in 1905 by a group of independent African merchants. It was taken over by the UAC in 1929 and changed its name to Export Buyers Ltd in 1955. In 1977 its name was changed again, this time to Liver Transport Ltd and it currently operates from 100, Old Hall Street, Liverpool. Unilever is the ultimate holding company of both of these firms. (See Henry Tyrer MSS, Box 49.)

47. I am indebted to Mr and Mrs R.L. Jones for their assistance with this section.

48. See below, Chapter 8, p. 115.

49. Henry Tyrer MSS, *Director's Minute Book,* no. 1, 29 January 1946, p. 202.

50. Henry Tyrer MSS, Box 6, letter from F. Cutts to F. Samuel, 9 March 1948.

51. Henry Tyrer MSS, *Director's Minute Book,* no. 1, 12 March 1948, p. 211.

52. Ibid., pp. 206, 210, 214 and 225.

53. Ibid., 30 March 1949, p. 214. Herbert Metcalf Warlow had joined the Company in 1897 at about the same time as Frederick Cutts and like Cutts he had been an original director when the firm acquired 'limited' status in 1914. Virtually all of his service had been at the Preston office.

54. Ibid., 31 March 1950, p. 225.

55. P.T. Bauer, *West African Trade* (Cambridge University Press, London, 1954), p. 200.

56. Davies, *The Trade Makers,* pp. 322-3.

57. Roger Kohn, *Palm Line: The Coming of Age, 1949-1970* (Palm Line Ltd, London, 1970), p. 26.

58. Ibid., p. 31.

59. Henry Tyrer MSS, *Director's Minute Book,* no. 1, 31 March 1950, p. 227.

60. Ibid.

61. Ibid., 31 March 1950, p. 227.

8   THE POST-WAR YEARS

I

The ending of the UAC agency, the loss of a substantial number of staff and the move to fresh premises all meant that the year 1950 marked a watershed in the activities undertaken by Henry Tyrer and Company Limited. The Chairman and Managing Director, Frederick Cutts, was turned seventy by this time but, nevertheless, he began the task of re-constructing the firm's fortunes with great enthusiasm. His work was aided by the remaining directors, Messrs D. Ollerton and G. Sanders at Liverpool, and by S. Dalzell, H.C. Lyon and J. Pilkington at Preston and under his guidance this experienced, but reduced, team soon proved that it was quite capable of meeting the new challenge.

The official termination of the link with the UAC was followed by the ending of the agreement whereby Freight Conveyors organised its stevedoring in Liverpool. As noted earlier[1] this activity had been arranged since 1937 in association with Liver Transport Limited but once the Agency ceased to operate the latter firm undertook all of Palm's cargo handling on its own account. This effectively meant a loss of 45% of the work previously carried out jointly by Freight Conveyors and Liver Transport,[2] but with the aid of some new customers, including Brown Geveke and Company, the firm was able to continue on a profitable basis throughout the 1950s and early 1960s.[3]

Mr Cutts' response to these changes had two distinct aspects. In the first place he sought to make his remaining agencies more efficient and attractive and by concentrating his attention on these existing accounts he was able to ensure that a very high standard was achieved. Cutts' early training when Tyrer's were in a small way of business had reinforced his own rather, cautious, nature so he was at his best in providing a meticulous service where mistakes were rare and never repeated. This style of operation gained Tyrer's an enviable reputation and the Company functioned like a well-oiled machine. Thus existing customers remained content and their personal recommendations encouraged many other potential clients to decide to sample Tyrer's facilities.

The search for new business was Mr Cutts' second response to the loss of the UAC agency but, while he had been highly successful in satisfying his traditional accounts, he found it difficult to meet the demands made by fresh trades. The changing conditions of the post-war world, together with the rapid developments in technology, were increasingly hard for him to appreciate at his advanced age. In these circumstances it was fortunate that he was prepared to allow his younger colleagues to accept some responsibility for certain of the developing trades, although it should be noted that he always kept the ultimate control in his own hands.

In the period from 1946 to 1949 Tyrer's main source of revenue had been from the UAC (42%), from general agency work at Liverpool and Preston (42%) and from its Coastwise and Transport Departments (16%).[4] Under Mr Cutts' supervision the remaining Liverpool agencies continued to flourish and earnings at Preston and from the handling of coastal vessels at both ports remained at a satisfactory level. The only problem was the gap created by the ending of the UAC work and here the Company was aided by the growth of a number of fresh interests.

Amongst the agencies already held was that for the India Steam Ship Company. This had originally been secured through Tyrer's contact with the London firm of Stelp and Leighton who were the general UK agents and this was ultimately confirmed during an interview between the chairman of the line, Sir Ramaswami Mudaliar, and Frederick Cutts. The agency was largely organised by Mr T.E.K. Wilson who had joined Tyrer's in 1948 from the Anchor Line and with his experience of the Indian East-bound trade it gradually provided a substantial amount of revenue. Another of Mr Wilson's[5] responsibilities was the agency for the Zim Line which had also been acquired in the late 1940s. This, too, generated a significant level of employment for Tyrer's were in charge of its growing loadings for Israel and other Mediterranean countries as well as its inward fruit shipments during the season. Of even greater potential importance was the agency for the Ben Line. The first Ben ship had been dealt with by Tyrer's in 1926 and, therefore, occasional vessels had been handled at infrequent intervals. The arrival of the 'Mac' ships during the Second World War[6] further strengthened this relationship and in the early post-war years Tyrer's always acted for the few Ben ships which came to Liverpool. These developments, together with the maintenance of existing trades at both Liverpool and Preston, enabled Henry Tyrer and Company to overcome the initial difficulties caused by the split from the Palm Line and then formed a useful basis for its future expansion.

II

In some respect it may be argued that the loss of the UAC agency was a 'blessing in disguise' for it forced Tyrer's to seek other outlets for its services. This is not to suggest that attempts at diversification would not have been made in any case for the Company – like its competitors – was always on the lookout for new business. Indeed, in the period which followed the ending of the Second World War many extra agencies had been secured. What it meant was that the search for fresh interests acquired a greater significance and no opportunity, however small, was neglected. The agency business is, of course, highly volatile as it corresponds very closely with the changing levels and directions of trade. The early post-war years were a time of considerable upheaval during which many existing routes expanded or declined while simultaneously additional links came into being and either flourished or failed. In these circumstances, numerous new opportunities became available and, during the 1950s and 1960s, some of these developed into substantial trades which more than offset the break with the Palm Line.

Frederick Cutts retained his control of Tyrer's for a further eighteen years after 1950 and during this long period many significant changes took place. The India Steam Ship Company was important for the whole of this time and Tyrer's interest in this trade was re-inforced in 1962 when the agency for the Shipping Corporation of India was also obtained. Unfortunately, the association with the Zim Line, which provided considerable work in the early 1950s, could not be continued after it introduced a service between Lisbon and Israel. This was because Tyrer's already represented the Portuguese Geral Line so the Zim agency was amicably transferred at Tyrer's instigation to Messrs Bahr, Behrend and Company. The Geral Line seldom sent ships to Liverpool but substantial cargoes were sent on its behalf to Lisbon via the Ellerman Line. This freight was arranged on through Bills of Lading and, after trans-shipment, it was carried on to the Portuguese African colonies by Geral's vessels. This trade remained important for over twelve years but then, as circumstances altered, it began to decline and came to an end in the late 1960s.[7]

Another longstanding account was with James Currie and Company of Edinburgh. This had been secured when sailings from Liverpool to Hamburg and Bremen had re-commenced after the war and was particularly useful in that it helped Tyrer's to obtain the agency for the Bugsier Line of Hamburg. This came about when Currie and Bugsier began to operate a joint service and, although the Currie Line subsequently withdrew from this arrangement (and eventually left the route), Tyrer's were able to maintain its links with Bugsier and have continued to act for the German firm to the present day.

Henry Tyrer's traditional interests in the importation of woodpulp and timber remained an essential aspect of the Company's business throughout Mr Cutts' period as Chairman and Managing Director. The paper making firm of Bowaters had become its main customer for wood-pulp and this was carried in the vessels of the Gorthon Line for many years. This business has changed substantially over the past decade, however, so that most of Bowater's cargoes are now carried in chartered vessels. Tyrer's remain as agents for these ships and continue to handle the occasional Gorthon vessel when it unloads at Bowater's wharf at Ellesmere Port.[8]

Timber, like woodpulp, was imported from both Scandinavia and North America. Canadian timber originated mainly from the west coast and was landed at Liverpool, Garston, Ellesmere Port and Manchester. At first Tyrer's acted for the Anglo Canadian Company on behalf of its U.K. Agents, Tatham Bromage of London but this firm gradually provided fewer cargoes for Merseyside leaving Seaboard Shipping Company of Vancouver as the main importers. Tyrer's obtained this latter agency through its long standing connection with Messrs Eggar, Forrester and Verner of London who are Seaboard's general UK representatives.[9] An additional, though separate, link with Canada was via the Canuk Line. This agency, which was also secured through the good offices of Tatham Bromage, was concerned with the carriage of grain and general cargoes from Montreal and the Great Lakes during the 1950s but, unlike the west coast timber trade, it failed to maintain its early promise.[10] The only connection between the east coast and west coast trades was that Tyrer's attempted, with some success, to obtain cargoes for their return voyages to Canada.

Tyrer's agency for the Ben Line had little real significance in 1950 although an occasional vessel was already discharging part cargoes at Liverpool. There was, however, a steady build-up in this trade so that one ship a month began to call on a regular basis and the quantity of freight rose to substantial proportions. Under the terms of its conference agreement the Ben Line was precluded from loading on the west coast of Britain at this time so Tyrer's work was solely concerned with incoming vessels. They were then asked to attempt the marketing of Ben's services to the Far East via east coast loading ports and such was the vigour and enthusiasm of Tyrer's response that the canvassing proved to be a great success. Consequently, a strong rapport developed between the two firms and this was further enhanced when Tyrer's provided highly satisfactory facilities for a new, direct, service from Hong Kong to Liverpool *circa* 1962.[11] In turn, these mutually beneficial arrangements ensured that Tyrer's were well placed to play a full part when the trade was containerised in the early 1970s.[12]

Not all of Tyrer's activities under Mr Cutts proved to be as viable as the agencies for the Ben Line and the India Steam Ship Company. By 1962 these two trades, together with the Pacific coast timber vessels, were providing the majority of the Company's business[13] but a number of other interests had either declined drastically or had failed completely. One of the latter was the Fruit Express Line of Oslo. In pre-war days this had operated a number of ships owned by Sigurd Herlofson and Bjorn Bjornstad in the California fruit trade. During the war they were mainly employed between the United States and United Kingdom carrying refrigerated cargoes such as butter and lard, their fast speed enabling them to sail outside the convoy system. The Liverpool connection was continued after the war when a service to the Canary Islands was commenced (outward with small parcels and return with tomatoes and bananas), but the venture came to a complete halt in the late 1940s.[14]

Another similar experience was with the Southern Whaling and Sealing Company.[15] This agency had provided useful employment and revenue in the 1920s and 1930s but came to an end in 1941 when the fleet was sold to Salvesen's of Leith.[16] When, however, whaling resumed after the war Tyrer's were able to act for Salvesen's as well as for United Whalers and the Union Whaling Company of Durban. All three firms operated factory ships in the Antarctic and these included *Southern Harvester* and *Southern Venturer* (Salvesen's), *Balaena* (United Whalers) and *Abraham Larsen* (Union Whaling). In addition, Tyrer's became managers of the *Busen Star* and *Busen Rollo* which were registered in London but which were owned by two companies based in St Helier. These were on time charter to Shell Petroleum and made annual voyages to the Antarctic delivering fuel oil to the floating factories and returning with whale oil and other by-products. All of these activities provided Tyrer's with a great deal of valuable (if smelly) employment until the late 1950s when British, Norwegian and South African interests were replaced by massive investments from the Soviet Union and Japan.

This decline in whaling was caused by economic forces over which Tyrer's had no control. This was also the case with the sailings formerly operated to southern Scotland for in the post-war world coastal shipping could not compete with road transport. The Scottish route was only of minor importance to the Company but its difficulties were symptomatic of the problems of the whole of the coastwise traffic and this was, of course, of major significance. Thus in the financial year ending in August 1950, Tyrer's Liverpool office handled 343 coastal vessels[17] but, in 1968, it dealt with only ten.[18]

Similar economic forces led to comparable changes in Tyrer's business on the River Ribble. In 1950, the basis of its activities there lay in the importation of woodpulp and timber from the Baltic, the cattle and general trades with Northern and Southern Ireland and the coastal services. As at Liverpool the coastwise traffic steadily declined so that whereas fifty-three ships were handled in 1950[19] only one required attention in 1968.[20] Another severe blow came in 1966 when Coast Lines decided to open their own office at Preston, for this had the effect of reducing Tyrer's Irish trade to much smaller proportions.[21] Fortunately the number of foreign-going vessels arriving at Preston continued at a consistently high level and Tyrer's office was able to produce good results. Even so, the narrowing of the Company's base was clearly making it very vulnerable to possible changes in its remaining activities, so on the death of Mr Cutts in 1968, the position at Preston was by no means as promising as it appeared.

In many ways this was also true of the Liverpool office and thus of the Company as a whole. Mr Cutts and his colleagues had been remarkably successful in overcoming the loss of the UAC agency and from 1950 to 1968 the number of ocean-going vessels handled by Tyrer's at both Liverpool and Preston had been consistently higher than in the 1940s.[22] While it is true that net profits never achieved the exceptional peaks of the early post-war years when over £14,000 was earned on two occasions[23] the Company was able to return satisfactory financial results throughout the period of Mr Cutts direction. These varied from a low of just under £4,000 in 1951 to a high of £11,056 in 1960 and were always sufficient to pay both the 6% Preference dividends and Ordinary dividends of 25%.[24]

Unfortunately, these undoubted achievements tend to obscure the unpalatable truth that having survived the difficulties of the early 1950s the Company had settled into a kind of comfortable routine. As Chairman and Managing Director, Mr Cutts must take the major responsibility for this malaise but he should not be criticised too harshly. He had joined Tyrer's in 1897 when the firm was a tiny one and for the following seventy-two years had given it his complete energy and devotion. Apart from his interest in his family, Mr Cutts' whole life revolved around the Company, even refusing or curtailing holidays which he thought were a waste of time.[25] He was already over seventy years of age when he was forced to re-organise the firm and having re-established Tyrer's on solid foundations he became progressively more reluctant to introduce further changes.

Thus as Mr Cutts got older he was more and more content to organise the business so that existing accounts received the very highest degree of priority. These were dealt with in a smart and efficient manner and gained the Company an enviable reputation. Mr Cutts was also prepared, albeit with some anxiety, to permit his fellow directors to enter into new trades and activities so long as they fell within what he regarded as the natural orbit of Tyrer's interests. This he interpreted as meaning anything that he fully understood but, in spite of his long experience, the changing condition of the 1960s meant that many areas of potential development could not be appreciated by him. The retirement of Sydney Dalzell and John Pilkington from Preston and of Dick Ollerton from Liverpool — all in 1960 — worsened this situation and the long illness and subsequent death of George Sanders in 1963 was a further severe blow. All of these directors had grown up under Mr Cutts and he knew their capabilities. He had less knowledge of the younger directors and consequently less confidence in their advice. As a result many opportunities were ignored or not properly investigated, reserves were not sensibly invested and many senior members of the staff became frustrated and were apprehensive for the long term future of the Company.

III

Frederick Cutts died in harness, as he would have wished, on 15 October 1968. His legacy was a well respected and viable firm which possessed substantial reserves and a highly experienced staff. Beneath this happy picture, however, lay a rather different reality. Tyrer's had enjoyed a long period of moderately profitable stability under Mr Cutts but this had been almost entirely based on the kind of traditional agency work that was already beginning to decline. Consequently, the Company's strength lay in precisely those areas which had no long-term future yet no serious attempt had been made to diversify into the growing bulk, container and vehicle trades.

In these circumstances a policy designed to lessen the Company's dependence upon its former activities should have been adopted at a much earlier date but it had not been possible to persuade Mr Cutts to take the necessary action. It was clear, therefore, that whoever was appointed to succeed him would be faced with the urgent task of changing the direction of the firm so that it could move into fresh fields of endeavour where, hopefully, expansion could take place. This implied that a series of difficult decisions would have to be taken so it was essential that a man of strong character as well as long experience be nominated — fortunately for the Company just such a man was available and was ready to accept the responsibility for Tyrer's future prosperity.

The new Chairman and Managing Director was Charles Wilson Harrison who had joined the Company in 1935.[26] Thereafter, apart from a period of military service[27] Mr Harrison had spent the whole of his business life with Tyrer's or its subsidiary, Freight Conveyors Limited. During this time he had worked his way through each of the firm's departments and had spent a long period actually on the docks under the strict supervision of Mr R.L. Jones. Consequently he had become thoroughly acquainted with all aspects of Tyrer's activities and had gradually emerged as a person well qualified for promotion. His reward for long periods of diligence and devotion to the Company's interest came in 1956[28] when he was appointed a director. This was followed by a further period of nine years hard work as a member of the Board and he then received the final seal of approval from that most exacting of taskmasters, Frederick Cutts, when in 1965 he became the Vice-Chairman of the firm.[29]

Charles Harrison was, of course, the son of Maud Harrison who was the daughter of Henry Tyrer's sister, Ann.[30] He was, therefore a great nephew of the founder of the firm and it might be thought that it was this connection that ensured his rise to power. Nothing could be further from the truth. It was undoubtedly true that Henry Tyrer was anxious to maintain his family's control of the firm and it was for this reason that he appointed his nephew, Thomas Wilson, to succeed him when he died.[31] But Henry Tyrer was a realist and Mr Wilson was nominated because he was not only a relative but was also an extremely capable businessman. When Mr Wilson died, Frederick Cutts became Chairman because, although not a relative, he was clearly the best man available. This principle was again applied on the death of Mr Cutts for the profitability — even the survival — of the firm was felt to be in some danger. Consequently, Mr Harrison was appointed to be Chairman and Managing Director because he could command the confidence of the Board and not because he happened to be a distant relative of Henry Tyrer.[32]

It should also be noted in this respect that Charles Harrison's promotion had to be approved by the Company's shareholders and that he and his immediate family possessed only a small portion of its ordinary capital. Thus his move to the top had to be on merit or not at all so when his elevation was confirmed at the next Annual General Meeting of the firm it was because it was felt that the interests of the shareholders were safe in his hands.[33] Subsequent events have shown that this was indeed a wise decision but in any event it should not be forgotten that every AGM provides an opportunity for the Chairman to be challenged to justify his policies. In the present context, however, although it has been ten years since Mr Harrison achieved control, no shareholder has found it necessary to avail himself of this facility.

It might be thought that Charles Harrison took over the running of Tyrer's at a particularly critical time because the previous year had seen the first trading loss since the Company was incorporated in 1914. In fact, this was not the case for the trading deficit had been caused by the closure of the Suez Canal and by a lengthy dock strike at Liverpool and by the time that Mr Harrison became Chairman these difficulties had been largely overcome. Consequently, his first year in control saw a return to viability and a net profit of £5,888 was achieved.[34] This was approximately the same as that before the Suez crisis and so might be regarded as quite satisfactory but the result did not deceive the new Chairman.

Charles Harrison understood that changes in the methods and directions of trade were seriously weakening the foundations of Tyrer's former prosperity and that a new approach was necessary after a long period of conservative, though efficient, management. Once in office, therefore, he undertook a survey of the firm's position and after careful consultation with his fellow directors came to the conclusion that Tyrer's must move away from its traditional activities and seek compensation in other, expanding, areas of business. The new Board saw quite clearly, even at that early stage, that a rapidly changing world called for a high degree of flexibility and that the best answer to uncertainty lay in the widening of the Company's operations. Of course they could not be sure which options would lead to successful developments but considered that a policy of diversification would give Tyrer's its best chance of survival. Thus, while not neglecting the opportunities already available within the Company, a positive search for profitable investments in other trades was actively organised and was to prove a characteristic of the ensuing decade.

IV

The death of Frederick Cutts in October 1968, saw the Company still very heavily engaged in what might best be described as its traditional activities. Thus at that time 'general ship agency work' at Liverpool provided 35% of its gross income and 'shipping and forwarding' were responsible for generating a further 9%. The Indian trade was the largest single interest and this supplied 27% of the firm's revenue, while the

German services earned an additional 6%. The Preston office was also a major source of income and contributed 31% of the total[35] but this, too, came almost entirely from trades which had changed very little over the years.

Over the next ten years this pattern of activity was to change quite dramatically. As a result 'general ship agencies and commissions' declined and provided only 14% of gross income while 'shipping and forwarding commissions' fell to under 6%. The contributions of the Indian and German agencies were also appreciably less, while the situation at Preston was even worse for by 1977 earnings there were only marginally over one per cent of total revenue.[36]

These somewhat gloomy statistics are, however, distorted by two distinct factors. In the first place all of these activities (with the exception of Preston office) actually produced more revenue in monetary terms but when inflation is taken into account this still meant a fall in real values. In the second place Tyrer's gross income rose by approximately 700% in the decade which followed the death of Mr Cutts. Consequently the growth of the Company's new interests tends to exaggerate the decline of its traditional trades when these are expressed as percentages of gross revenue. Nevertheless it is quite clear that Tyrer's former business fell away significantly during this period so that by 1977 its previous activities were providing only a third of total gross income.[37]

The reduction in Tyrer's customary agency work at Liverpool was a consequence of the changes in technology that were moving the whole of the shipping industry away from conventional methods of operation. More and more cargoes were being transported by specialised bulk carriers, while palletisation and containerisation were eating away at traditional dry cargo shipments. In turn, this affected other aspects of Tyrer's business so that less and less shipping and forwarding was available. These difficulties were also present at Preston but there they were complicated and compounded by a series of other changes.

The port of Preston had reached a peak in the late 1950s and had then commenced a long period of slow decline.[38] The ending of Tyrer's Irish agencies in 1966[39] and the virtual cessation of its coastal business[40] had already created problems in Mr Cutts' day but the buoyancy of other services had enabled the profitability of the Preston office to be maintained. A dock strike, which lasted for ten weeks during 1969, then caused trade to be diverted to other ports and some of this never returned. This was particularly important to Tyrer's as it brought to an end Everard's Swedish service which had previously brought woodpulp, timber and general cargo into the port, taking stone from Llandulas back to Scandinavia.[41] It also encouraged firms like Price and Pierce (Woodpulp) Limited to operate through Hartlepool instead of Preston for the opening of the motorway system meant that paper mills in Lancashire could conveniently be supplied from the east coast. The saving of some 400 miles on the sea route would have made this development likely in any event, but the industrial disruption at Preston ensured that it was introduced at the earliest possible date.[42]

During the past ten years, therefore, Tyrer's have suffered from the general deterioration of trade at Preston and have been especially hit by the collapse of the woodpulp imports which had previously formed a major part of their business. The Company had also felt the effect of the reduction in the Scandinavian timber business for this, too, had formerly provided substantial revenues. Paradoxically the labour difficulties which had helped to drive trade away from Preston has sometimes been responsible for bringing it back. Thus the diversion of ships from other strike-torn ports has occasionally supplied some welcome, additional, cargoes. For the most part, however, Tyrer's have had to depend upon the regular services operated to the Mediterranean by Moss Hutchison and Ellerman City Lines (now recently terminated) and on the infrequent shipments of Scandinavian timber and woodpulp and French wheat which arrive at intermittent intervals.

The whole future of the port of Preston is currently under review and it appears improbable, even if it survives, that it can ever again provide Tyrer's with a principal outlet for these services. The diminishing value of the Preston office together with the decrease in the Company's traditional activities at Liverpool emphasise still further the importance of the developments that were initiated after the death of Frederick Cutts in 1968.

V

Throughout the post-war period Tyrer's had played an important part in the Indian trade. The Company's relationship with the India Steam Ship Company and the Shipping Corporation of India had traditionally been very close and these agencies had proved to be mutually beneficial for a long period. Over the years many officials and representatives had been received and made welcome at Liverpool and Mr T.E.K. Wilson had visited India in 1963.[43] Charles Harrison appreciated the value of these personal contacts so it was arranged that he, together with the Vice-Chairman (Mr J.E. Lyon), should undertake a further visit. This was completed during 1973 and as a result of the renewal or establishment of the friendships which this encouraged both sides now have a much fuller understanding of the others difficulties and aspirations.

Similarly, the Company has placed great value on its connection with the Bugsier Line and, during the past twenty years, have maintained a specially close relationship to their joint advantage. But the volume of business generated by the Indian and German agencies was insufficient, in itself, to do more than provide some stability to Tyrer's affairs during a period of constant change. In fact, of all the agencies which survived from Tyrer's traditional activities it was that of the Ben Line that was eventually to provide the largest element in the expansion of the Company.

As noted earlier, Tyrer's links with William Thomson and Company, the Managers of the Ben Line, dated back to the 1920s.[44] In the course of time this connection developed into a small but valuable agency under which one ship per month was handled on a regular basis. This was purely for incoming cargo but Tyrer's also canvassed for custom for outward shipments which, in accordance with the conference agreements of the time, had to be exported from east coast ports.[45] The success of these arrangements strengthened the relationship between the two firms and encouraged the establishment of a direct service from Hong Kong in the early 1960s.[46] However, the real reward for Tyrer's efficiency and the confidence with which they were held by Thomson's came in 1971 for they were then appointed as agents for the newly organised Ben Line Containers Limited, with responsibility for the whole of the North West area of the country.[47]

The containerisation of the Far East trade necessitated a large expenditure in the opening, staffing and furnishing of offices at Manchester and Aintree Container bases[48] and it took several years to become fully operational. By 1973, however, the new system was handling very substantial quantities of cargo in both directions and the returns were clearly sufficient to offset the additional costs and more than compensated for the loss of the conventional Ben Line services to Liverpool.[49] Since then, under the guidance of Mr Rodney Kaye, the throughput of Ben Line Containers has continued to grow and it now provides a significant proportion of Tyrer's revenue.[50] It is interesting to note that the very changes in technology which had destroyed so much of the Company's former business has, in this case, worked to its advantage. Thus, in the long-term, Tyrer's position has been strengthened not weakened by post-war innovations but this is only true because under Charles Harrison's leadership the Company has been prepared to invest and grasp its opportunities as they arose.

This was particularly evident in Tyrer's diversification into timber distribution and road haulage. The Company had, of course, been interested in the importation of timber at both Liverpool and Preston for many years[51] but in the mid-sixties the introduction of bulk carriers threatened to alter the whole structure of the trade. Consequently, the Liverpool timber merchants set up a committee in association with the Mersey Dock and Harbour Board and this recommended that special facilities be established.[52] Unfortunately the only available site for a timber terminal was at No 3 Canada Dock. This had adequate draught but it possessed only three acres of quay space. It was quickly appreciated that an area of this size could only cater for bulk shipments of timber if the incoming cargoes were removed from the site very rapidly. This pre-supposed some new form of efficient organisation and as a first step towards this development the Timber Merchants agreed to give up their long-standing right to collect their own imports from the docks.

There the matter rested and Tyrer's became concerned that if no action was taken it might lead to their clients diverting their vessels to other UK ports. Acting primarily as agents for the Canadian Seaboard organisation, Tyrer's then approached the Transport Development Group but failed to persuade it to undertake the project.[53] The Company subsequently attempted to interest several other bodies but all refused and it was only after considerable effort that the Liverpool Depot of British Road Services finally agreed to become involved.

British Road Services never, in fact, provided enough vehicles to move the timber quickly enough so Rodney Kaye, in close collaboration with David Harrison, were forced to take a considerable interest in the terminal. Tyrer's main concern was to ensure that its ships were not detained so when the quay became congested from lack of vehicles Mr Kaye introduced contract hire lorries. This meant, in practice, that British Road Services made considerable profits while Tyrer's did most of the administration. In order to put this arrangement on a more regular basis Tyrer's then became sub-contractors and received a commission on each transaction they organised. This gradually evolved into a satisfactory system and as it had the approval of both the Mersey Dock and Harbour Board and the timber trade, it became a permanent feature of the firm's activities.

Tyrer's involvement with the organisation of road transport then suggested that this might provide a suitable opportunity for further diversification. Consequently, in September 1970, Speed Haulage Limited was incorporated so that the Company could take a direct part in the distribution of the timber.[54] At that time the Tyrer personnel concerned with these developments, Rodney Kaye and David Harrison, had little practical knowledge of actually operating road transport. It was arranged, therefore, that Messrs D.R. Pass and Company of Southport would provide drivers and would also licence, maintain and garage the vehicles for an initial period.[55] In the first instance, only one second hand unit and trailer was purchased. This had the effect of reducing any possible loss in what was a completely fresh activity to small proportions and three new units were acquired once the investment was seen to be justified.[56] This involved heavy capital outlay but with the growth of expertise was considered by the Chairman to be an acceptable risk.[57]

From 1970, therefore, Tyrer's were involved with both the organisation of timber distribution from the Liverpool terminal and with the actual carriage of a small proportion of the total throughput. This situation was, however, significantly changed when, at the end of 1971, British Road Services decided to withdraw their facilities.[58] This came about because of their decision to close their Liverpool Depot which, overall, was running at a loss. Tyrer's were placed in a difficult position by this development and attempted, unsuccessfully, to persuade a number of private hauliers to enter the trade. A further attempt to interest the Warrington Depot of British Road Services also failed so the Company felt obliged to set up its own organisation.[59]

The Liverpool timber trade and the Mersey Dock and Harbour Company[60] were reluctant to accept this change but in the absence of any immediate alternative they agreed to give it a trial. They were influenced in the beginning by the fact that British Road Services had withdrawn quite voluntarily but later accepted the new arrangement on its merits when it was seen that Tyrer's were not seeking to exploit their additional role. Consequently when the timber terminal was moved from Canada to Seaforth Dock in July 1973, Tyrer's were authorised to continue their regulation of the trade.

Since then all bulk shipments of timber into Liverpool have been distributed via the facilities provided by Henry Tyrer and Company. This involves considerable administrative work for all landings have to be linked with the appropriate transport and the whole operation requires close co-operation with the Mersey Dock and Harbour Company and the importers. Tyrer Transport Services[61] are responsible for organising this side of the business and utilise their own as well as hired vehicles to effect the distribution. Over the years its own fleet has gradually been expanded so that by 1975 the firm owned six sets of tractors and trailers and these were used almost entirely in the movement of timber. Further progress was made at the end of 1976 when a road haulage depot situated at Rimrose Road, Bootle, was purchased from Pearson (Hauliers) Limited.[62] This has since enabled Tyrer's to sever their connection with Mr Pass and it now operates as a completely independent unit. It is also a further step on the road towards complete diversification into general haulage for Charles Harrison is quite convinced that the Company must keep moving forward and this possibility can now always be considered. In the meanwhile the possession of this property has meant that Tyrer Transport Services, under the direction of David Harrison, have a firm base from where its drivers can work conveniently and where its own employees can repair and maintain what is a still increasing fleet of tractors and trailers.[63]

Tyrer's responsibility for the distribution of Liverpool's bulk timber imports now forms an important part of the firm's total activities and, together with the earnings of Tyrer Transport Services, makes a significant contribution to its revenue. Both of these developments have come to fruition during Charles Harrison's period as Chairman and, although the original proposals may have been suggested by others, he ultimately took the final decisions and must, therefore, receive most of the credit. On the same grounds Mr Harrison must accept the blame for the failure of the Company's other major attempt at diversification even though he was not the prime mover in the enterprise.

This second development was an attempt to enter into the retail food business. Tyrer's had no special expertise in this trade but, acting on what appeared to be sound advice, premises were leased at Wigan[64] and Speed Foods Limited was incorporated in September 1970[65] The rationale behind this move was that under Mr Cutts substantial reserves had been built up but had not been invested to obtain the maximum return. The new Board had quickly improved the Company's portfolio[66] but it still seemed sensible to use these idle funds to widen the firm's base and also obtain a better return on its capital.

In the event, however, neither of these objectives were achieved. It rapidly became apparent that the operation of a supermarket required far more knowledge of the food trade than had been anticipated. This could, of course, have been remedied in time but it would have meant that at least one of the senior directors would have had to be diverted from his other duties on a permanent basis. This would then have led to a reduction of efficiency elsewhere and perhaps to a general re-organisation that might have disturbed the whole balance of what was, after all, a highly successful firm. After only one year's operation, therefore, it was decided that expert advice should be sought and when this confirmed that the investment was unlikely to prove profitable it was agreed that the store should be disposed of on the best terms that could be arranged.[67]

An agreement was then entered into with Messrs James Hall and Company of Southport under which this firm undertook to manage the business until such time as it could be sold.[68] For a variety of reasons the sale of the Wigan supermarket took far longer to arrange than had been anticipated and it is only now, at the end of 1978, that the disposal is being finalised.[69] Fortunately, however, part of the original capital outlay was recovered in 1971 and, with the aid of the agreement made with Hall's, subsequent annual losses have been kept to very small proportions.

The losses suffered by Tyrer's in respect of Speed Foods Limited are to be regretted but in some ways they have served a useful purpose. The concept of diversification adopted by the firm after 1968 was undoubtedly, with the benefit of hindsight, the right one for without it the Company would by now have been reduced to chasing ever decreasing amounts of traditional agency work. Instead an examination of the overall results that have been achieved during the past nine years shows that turnover has risen from £108,538 in 1967-8 to £723,031 in 1976-7[70] and further analysis indicates that at least two-thirds of this is attributable to the new activities generated by the Board of Directors since the death of Mr Cutts. Thus the failure of one specific investment has been massively compensated by the success of the overall policy and, in addition, the Company now appreciates that for diversification to be viable it needs to build on, or be linked to, some aspect of its current business. Any future plans will, therefore take notice of this hard-earned lesson — that it is wise to confine one's interests within the spheres of one's reasonable knowledge.[71]

VI

The Company founded by Henry Tyrer one hundred years ago still bears his mark. Thus in spite of the tremendous progress made in recent years the Chairman is still to be found insisting that the directors must '. . . keep a sharp watch for any other viable interests.'[72]

It is clear, therefore, that Henry Tyrer's own attitude to expansion has been rekindled during the present regime and many new activities have been instigated. Apart from those developments described above, these have included a number of fresh agencies of which at least two are promising substantial business for the future. The importation of cars from Italy into Preston is one such trade. This began in 1972 as a relatively small operation and has now grown to such a scale that it has had to be transferred to Merseyside where large numbers of Fiats are now brought into Ellesmere Port and Birkenhead. At first, Car Line of Paris returned in ballast but a marketing survey instigated by Charles Harrison suggested a large potential for traffic, particularly vehicles, destined for Mediterranean ports. This has since proved to be the case and the business has built up to such an extent that the Company ordered a larger and more sophisticated vessel which now provides a service for the export of heavy agricultural and excavating machinery.

Another similar growth point is supplied by the Algerian CNAN Line which operates a fortnightly service from Garston to North Africa. This carries mainly lube oil and general cargo outward but there is little in the way of imports from Algeria. However, the potential for such a trade is quite considerable and if and when it occurs the Company will be well placed to offer its facilities with its customary enthusiasm.

It should be noted that the CNAN agency was obtained through Tyrer's long standing connection with Messrs Killick Martin of London who, of course, are Ben Line's loading brokers for the UK. Killick Martin were also responsible for the appointment of Tyrer's to act as agents for NORCO and Lykes Lines at Liverpool.[73]

This search for new opportunities is just one aspect of the very positive attitude which now characterises Tyrer's operations. Another indication is suggested by the manner in which the difficulties encountered by Speed Foods were resolved. Once it was realised that this enterprise was likely to be unproductive an immediate decision was made to withdraw as quickly as possible. There was no attempt to disguise the fact that a mistake had been made and, consequently, the Company was able 'to cut its losses' in a very effective way. Yet a further feature of Tyrer's fresh approach since the death of Mr Cutts has been the acceptance of new technology and of the need to utilise its resources in a less rigid manner. Thus Telex is now widely used and space is rented so that a computer produces manifests and related documents for the Indian service.[74] It should also be noted that the Company moved to 'new and more prestigeous offices'[75] at Reliance House in the middle of Liverpool's commercial centre in 1974. This was indeed a far cry from Henry Tyrer's motto of 'Look after the pennies and the pounds will look after themselves . . .' but in the event has proved to be a true economy as well as being mutually beneficial to both the Company and its customers.

Of even greater significance than these events, however, has been the change in the attitude towards the directors and staff. Charles Harrison's very first decision after being appointed Chairman was to ensure that Mr G.E. Stretch, the Company's Secretary, be promoted to the Board.[76]

He then went on to stress that he saw his position as being that of leader of a team in which all would play a full part in establishing the policy of the Company.[77] Since then it has been Tyrer's intention to reward talent and industry and many employees throughout the enterprise have been inspired to follow in the footsteps of G.B. Hannan, D.C. Harrison and G. Wall who were all made assistant directors in October 1968.[78] The introduction of a new pension scheme which started in 1969[79] together with good working conditions and an improved salary structure have all helped to improve relationships within the firm and the net result has been a relatively content and hence an extremely efficient staff.

All of Mr Harrison's plans and efforts would, of course, have been of little avail without the loyal support of his senior colleagues. James Edward Lyon (Junior) who had joined the Company in 1933[80] and who had been made a director in 1961 acted as Vice-Chairman from 1968 until his retirement in 1978. This was the period when Tyrer's fortunes were completely transformed and Mr Lyon played a full part in supporting the changes introduced by his Chairman. Charles Harrison clearly relied upon him both as advisor and friend and at the 58th Annual General Meeting '. . . wished to record both his own and the Company's appreciation of the energy and devotion shown by Mr Lyon, not only in the Indian business, but also in connection with BLC and in general Company matters . . .'[81]

The other senior members of the Board[82] during this vital decade were Rodney Kaye (appointed a director in 1965), John Lea (who was promoted in 1961), John Sanders (who joined the Board in 1956) and George Stretch who, as noted above, had been made a director in 1968. This group, together with Gordon Hannan and David Harrison who were made 'full' directors in 1976, have provided a very real and effective management of the Company and since 1975 this has been further strengthened by the recruitment of Mr Bernard Dowd as Company Secretary.

The first Company Secretary was Mr Walter Stretch and he served in this position from 1914 when the Company was incorporated to 1937 when he retired after many years service. Mr Joseph Meagher was then appointed and, apart from a short break due to illness,[83] he acted as Company Secretary until his retirement in 1961. G.E. Stretch then took over and continued in this capacity for over nine years. It was then considered that the increasing size of the firm warranted a full-time Secretary and Mr H. Reid, an accountant who had worked within the Company for a number of years, was appointed to fill this position.[84]

Five years later Mr Reid tendered his resignation and Charles Harrison, personally, set about finding a replacement with past secretarial experience. A number of fully qualified candidates who had held similar positions with first class companies were then interviewed, and Mr B.J. Dowd was eventually selected.[85] This has been proved by events to have been a wise and correct choice and Mr Dowd now enters into all discussions which relate to the well being of the Company and the welfare of the staff as well as fulfilling his prime role as a financial and legal adviser. He has become, in short, a well respected member of the management team.

It is as the leader of this team that Charles Harrison sees his role as Chairman of Henry Tyrer and Company. His decade in authority has been marked by a 'consultative' as distinct from a 'dictatorial' style although he has readily accepted full responsibility for all Board decisions. The profitability of the past ten years during a period of unprecedented change bears witness to his undoubted ability and this has been recognised in a wider context by his nomination as the next Chairman of the Liverpool Steamship Owners Association. This is a most unusual honour for the representative of a firm which does not operate its own vessels and demonstrates quite remarkably the regard in which he is held by the shipping community.

Henry Tyrer and Company Limited, is now set to embark on its second century. Its creation in a tiny office in the centre of Liverpool during 1879 was followed by a period of uncertainty but by 1897, when Frederick Cutts and Herbert Warlow joined the staff of four, it was firmly established on what were to prove sound foundations. Thereafter Henry Tyrer continued to innovate and seek new outlets for his enterprise and with the aid of Henry Drain, James Edward Lyon (Senior), George Sanders, Walter Stretch and Thomas Wilson he secured 'Limited' status in 1914 and so placed the firm on a wider footing. Then, in spite of advancing age, Henry Tyrer successfully overcame the difficulties of the post-war slump and by the time of his death in 1936 his Company was well respected and active in a large number of trades.

Thomas Wilson and Frederick Cutts consolidated these achievements and provided a highly efficient management structure. However, when the latter died in 1968 it became apparent that changes in technology and in the methods of trade were undermining the Company's traditional business. In these circumstances the Board of Directors, under the guidance of Charles Harrison, decided upon a policy of diversification. This has been extremely successful so that the number of staff has risen from the forty of 1968 to over one hundred today, while Tyrer's assets and reserves have also grown quite dramatically. The business that is now being conducted from Liverpool, Preston, Bootle, Seaforth and Manchester, would surely have pleased and amazed its founder and the expertise of the present management together with the skill of the current staff suggest that the progress made in recent years will continue into the foreseeable future.

Notes

1. See above, Chapter 7, p. 110.
2. Henry Tyrer MSS, Box 32, interviews with Mr R.L. Jones, 14 July 1977 and 26 July 1978.
3. Ibid., Box 46, the Devlin Committee on 'matters concerning the Ports Transport' (HMSO, Cmmd 2734, 1965) recommended that the number of stevedoring companies in Liverpool be reduced to ten. Accordingly, Freight Conveyors amalgamated with Mersey Ports to form Freight Conveyors Mersey Port Stevedoring Limited. This operated until 1968 when the business was sold to the Mersey Dock and Harbour Company. Freight Conveyors Limited, which had remained in being as a holding company, was then liquidated. The sum of £96,481 was then returned to its shareholders, i.e. £23 per £1 share, so the Company had obviously made substantial profits during its years in business.
4. Ibid., Box 34, Analysis of Sources of Revenue by Mr H. Fair of Messrs Warlow and Fair, Accountants to Henry Tyrer and Co Ltd.
5. T.E.K. Wilson esq was of Scottish origin. He was not a relative of the other Wilsons in the Company.
6. The 'Mac' ships were merchant aircraft carriers which made regular voyages from the United States and Canada. They carried planes on deck which were used for convoy escort duty. These flew off as the vessels approached the Mersey — the bulk cargoes of grain were then discharged in Alexandra Dock. See above, Chapter 7, p. 105.
7. Henry Tyrer MSS, *Director's Minute Book,* no. 2, 29 March 1968, p. 51.
8. The Gorthon Line still plays an important role in the pulp trade but most of their business is with other ports.
9. These connections were to have important consequences in the future. See below, pp. 126-7.
10. Henry Tyrer MSS, *Director's Minute Book,* no. 1, 18 March 1955, p. 247.
11. Henry Tyrer MSS, Box 48, interview with Mr R. Kaye, 30 July 1978.
12. See below, p. 126.
13. Henry Tyrer MSS, *Director's Minute Book,* no. 2, 22 March 1963, p. 22.
14. Henry Tyrer MSS, Box 37, interview with D. Ollerton, 29 November 1977.
15. See above, Chapter 6, p. 82 and Chapter 7, p. 104.
16. Henry Tyrer MSS, Box 22.
17. Henry Tyrer MSS, *Director's Minute Book,* no. 1, 30 March 1951, p. 234.
18. Ibid., no. 2, 6 March 1969, p. 57.
19. Ibid., no. 1, 30 March 1951, p. 234.
20. Ibid., no. 2, 6 March 1969, p. 57.
21. Ibid., 12 March 1967, p. 42.
22. See Appendix, Table 9, p. 146.
23. This was in 1949 and 1950.
24. See Appendix, Table 6, pp. 142-3.

25. Author's interview with Mr Cutts in 1965.

26. See above, Chapter 6, p. 95.

27. Charles Harrison was a member of the pre-war Territorial Army so he was called to the colours just prior to the beginning of hostilities. He subsequently served in France with the 59th Medium Regiment, Royal Artillery, and after being wounded was evacuated via Dunkirk. His injuries necessitated a long period of convalescence before he was invalided out of the Army and he then returned to Tyrer's in 1941.

28. Henry Tyrer MSS, *Director's Minute Book*, no. 1, 16 March 1956, p. 251.

29. Ibid., no. 2, 28 September 1965, p. 37.

30. See Appendix, Table 1, p. 137.

31. See above, Chapter 7, pp. 101-2.

32. Henry Tyrer MSS, *Director's Minute Book*, no. 2, 28 October 1968, p. 52.

33. Ibid., 6 March 1969, p. 56.

34. Ibid., 6 March 1969, p. 57.

35. Henry Tyrer MSS, Box 34, Analysis of Sources of Revenue by Mr H. Fair of Messrs Warlow and Fair, Accountants to Henry Tyrer and Co Ltd.

36. Ibid. This, however, should be regarded as an unduly low figure.

37. Ibid.

38. See Appendix, Table 4, p. 140.

39. See above, p. 120.

40. Ibid.

41. Henry Tyrer MSS, Box 48, interview with Mr K. Dalzell, 29 September 1978.

42. Ibid., Box 33, interview with Mr N. Harris, 9 August 1977.

43. Henry Tyrer MSS, *Director's Minute Book*, no. 2, 20 March 1964, p. 29.

44. See above, p. 116.

45. Ibid., p. 118.

46. Ibid.

47. Henry Tyrer MSS, *Director's Minute Book*, no. 2, 18 February 1972, p. 88.

48. Ibid. One consequence of the establishment of a new office at the Manchester Container base was the decision to close the Company's premises at Tower Chamber, Spring Gardens, in the centre of Manchester. This had been opened in 1960 and, under the guidance of Mr G. Wall, had proved to be a valuable asset to Tyrer's business. See also Chapter 6, p. 80.

49. Ibid., 21 February 1974, p. 98.

50. Henry Tyrer MSS, Box 34, Analysis of Sources of Revenue by Mr H. Fair of Messrs Warlow and Fair, Accountants to Henry Tyrer and Co Ltd.

51. See above, p. 118.

52. Henry Tyrer MSS, Box 48, interview with Mr. R. Kaye, 30 July 1978.

53. Ibid.

54. Henry Tyrer MSS, *Director's Minute Book*, no. 2, 11 February 1971, p. 77.

55. Henry Tyrer MSS, Box 48, interview with Mr R. Kaye, 30 July 1978.

56. Ibid., interview with Mr D. Harrison, 26 July 1978.

57. Author's interview with C.W. Harrison, 25 October 1978.

58. Henry Tyrer MSS, *Director's Minute Book*, no. 2, 11 January 1973, p. 93.

59. Henry Tyrer MSS, Box 48, interview with Mr R. Kaye, 30 July 1978.

60. The Mersey Dock & Harbour *Board* became the Mersey Dock & Harbour *Company* in 1972.

61. Speed Haulage Limited, was re-named Tyrer Transport Services Limited, in September 1973.

62. Henry Tyrer MSS, *Director's Minute Book*, no. 2, 5 August 1976, p. 120.

63. The current (1978) fleet consists of fifteen tractors and sixteen trailers.

64. Henry Tyrer MSS, *Director's Minute Book,* no. 2, 29 July 1970, p. 68.

65. Ibid., 11 February 1971, p. 77.

66. Ibid., 6 December 1968, p. 54.

67. Ibid., 18 May 1971, p. 80.

68. Ibid., agreement dated 9 July 1971, p. 83.

69. Henry Tyrer MSS, Box 29, Statement by Chairman to 64th Annual General Meeting held on 16 February 1978.

70. Ibid., Box 34, Analysis of Sources of Revenue by Mr H. Fair of Messrs Warlow and Fair, Accountants to Henry Tyrer and Co Ltd.

71. Author's interview with C.W. Harrison, 25 October 1978.

72. Henry Tyrer MSS, *Director's Minute Book,* no. 2, 21 February 1974, p. 99.

73. Discussions with Mr J.F. Sanders, 9 November 1978. See also: D.R. Macgregor, *The China Bird. The History of Captain Killick and 100 Years of Sail and Steam* (Chatto & Windus, London, 1961).

74. Henry Tyrer MSS, *Director's Minute Book,* no. 2, 17 December 1975, p. 114.

75. Ibid., 30 January 1975, p. 104.

76. Ibid., 28 October 1968, p. 53.

77. Ibid.

78. Ibid.

79. Ibid., 6 March 1969, p. 58.

80. See above, Chapter 6, p. 95.

81. Henry Tyrer MSS, *Director's Minute Book,* no. 2, 18 February 1972, p. 87.

82. See Appendix, Table 10, pp. 147-8. Note that Mr W.P. Searle was appointed a director in 1965 but died suddenly in August 1969.

83. Mr George Sanders acted as Company Secretary while Mr Meagher was ill during 1946.

84. Henry Tyrer MSS, *Director's Minute Book,* no. 2, 2 October 1970, p. 70.

85. Ibid., 7 October 1975, p. 113.

Table 1: Henry Tyrer's Family Tree

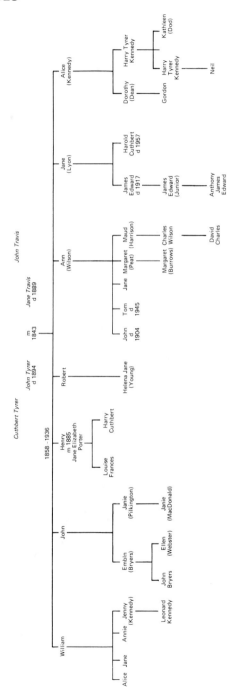

Table 2: Exports from British West Africa to the United Kingdom, 1854-1913

Commodity	1854 %	1884 %	1900 %	1913 %
Palm oil	40.2	53.9	40.7	39.5
Nuts for oil	3.0	25.9	12.5	15.4
Cocoa	—	—	—	9.9
Tin ore	—	—	—	8.3
Timber	36.4	—	14.4	8.2
Rubber	—	12.8	27.4	4.7
Other raw materials	—	—	—	4.3
Cotton	—	1.3	—	3.3
Manufactured articles	—	—	—	1.4
Grain, corn and maize	—	—	—	1.0
Gold	—	—	—	.5
Ivory	.6	1.1	1.2	.3
Gum	2.5	1.9	.5	.1
Ginger	3.1	1.1	.9	.1
Wax	7.9	.2	.1	.05
All other items	6.3	1.8	1.8	2.95
	100.0	100.0	100.0	100.0
Total values:	£252,814	£1,099,256	£2,137,023	£5,173,553[1]

1. Details of the trade of British West Africa with Britain are given in the 'Annual Statements of the Trade of the United Kingdom with Foreign Countries and British Possessions', published by HMSO. A comprehensive list of the value and weight of the principal commodities is given, but due to changes in political boundaries it would be unwise to compare the individual totals of the separate colonies with earlier or later years. A further complication is caused by the fact that many of the commodities arriving in Britain were without a specific port of origin, and were shown as 'not particularly designated', and were thus not included in the totals of imports from British possessions. The best available guide to the intricacies of West African trade statistics is that provided in the Statistical Appendices, 1880 to 1914, provided in C.W. Newbury, *British Policy towards West Africa, Select Documents 1875-1914* (London, Oxford University Press, 1971).

Table 3: Port of Preston Trade Statistics, 1884-1938

Year	No. of vessels	Registered tonnage	Imports Merchandise tons	Animals	Exports tons	Gross income	Working expenses	Profit & Loss Account: Deficiency	Surplus
1884	145	10,065	16,881	—	14,082	£ 2,261	£ 592	£ —	£ 1,169
1893	437	48,821	69,033	—	25,109	6,971	16,319	9,348	—
1894	1,046	121,365	191,846	—	28,313	14,650	21,256	6,606	—
1899	1,167	148,210	273,748	—	101,061	28,209	26,057	—	2,152
1904	1,482	236,551	448,174	—	147,624	51,904	42,969	—	8,935
1909	1,589	276,374	498,572	3,531	175,450	64,911	49,661	—	15,250
1914	1,481	294,884	530,251	59	213,339	76,963	57,118	—	19,845
1919	434	51,859	82,805	—	67,687	46,262	55,942	9,680	—
1924	1,463	400,428	497,747	30,230	432,013	216,874	175,913	—	40,961
1929	1,087	397,244	588,536	58,308	171,909	216,590	166,867	—	49,723
1934	1,395	583,112	751,784	57,509	176,100	228,519	165,528	—	62,991
1938	1,635	609,708	870,262	38,936	317,128	267,832	186,926	—	80,906

Based on: J. Barron, *A History of the Ribble Navigation from Preston to the Sea* (Guardian Press, Preston 1938), p. 409. (Abstract Statement of Trade of the Port of Preston since the Corporation became Sole Owners.)

Table 4: Port of Preston Trade Statistics, 1938-77

Year	Number of vessels	Gross registered tonnage	Tonnes imported	Tonnes exported	Total tonnes imports & exports
1938	1,494	560,095*	707,641	313,729	1,021,370
1948	1,767	603,095*	479,108	520,874	999,982
1958	2,196	1,431,328*	956,902	647,004	1,603,906
1975	1,385	623,737*	595,503	660,321	1,255,824
1976	1,003	482,513*	557,509	435,724	993,233
1977	774	610,815	592,026	401,480	993,506

	Imports (in tonnes)*					
	1938	1948	1958	1975	1976	1977
Unit loads — Irish	—	1,981	250,467	220,418	102,695	91,754
Unit loads — others	—	—	—	139,467	132,134	119,686
Bulk liquids	180,090	214,345	282,667	134,624	206,895	280,970
Woodpulp	181,486	88,076	218,494	26,090	28,241	25,391
Timber	87,871	34,357	47,184	16,153	16,204	13,159
Bulk solids	112,775	44,703	84,244	33,382	33,597	30,758
General	145,419	95,646	24,770	25,369	37,743	30,298
Bananas	—	—	49,076	—	—	—

	Exports (in tonnes)**					
	1938	1948	1958	1975	1976	1977
Unit loads — Irish	—	5,156	282,109	411,867	225,750	178,831
Unit loads — others	—	—	—	129,162	145,453	137,778
Coal & coke	282,399	422,857	332,541	26,071	880	379
Bulk liquids	10,667	25,007	24,854	4,789	785	110
General	18,194	67,854	6,992	35,726	35,171	28,836
Metal scrap	2,469	—	508	52,705	27,685	55,546

Based on traffic data supplied by the Port of Preston Authority, Dock Office, Preston, January 1978.

*　Net registered tonnage
** These figures are metric

Table 5: Vessels visiting the Port of Liverpool, 1879-1977

Year ending 1 July	Number of ships	Net registered tonnage
1879	18,420	7,034,356
1884	23,940	8,800,362
1889	22,662	9,291,964
1894	21,170	9,960,902
1899	25,522	12,534,116
1904	25,400	15,626,241
1909	24,799	16,747,479
1914	24,756	19,086,672
1919	12,372	12,324,010
1924	20,848	18,574,144
1929	20,583	20,521,906
1934	17,499	19,969,354
1939	18,378	21,724,050
1944	12,422	18,874,733
1949	15,388	19,575,035
1954	9,856	18,000,000
1959	9,869	19,549,000
1964	10,728	21,975,000
1969	8,262	19,322,000
1974	5,618	20,250,000
1977	5,369	31,883,000*

Note: Details for the years 1879 to 1949 inclusive were obtained from Stuart Mountfield's *Western Gateway, a History of the Mersey Docks and Harbour Board* (Liverpool University Press, 1965), pp. 204-5. The remaining figures were provided by the Marketing Department of the Mersey Docks and Harbour Company.

* Gross registered tonnage

Table 6: Annual Results of Henry Tyrer & Co Ltd

Year ending	Net profit[1] £	Preference dividends[2]	Ordinary dividends[2]	Notes
30 April 1915	902	6%	6%	
30 April 1916	1,322	6%	6%	
30 April 1917	3,729	6%	8%	
30 April 1918	3,150	6%	8%	
30 April 1919	2,808	6%	8%	
30 April 1920	8,083	6%	10%	
30 April 1921	7,417	6%	10%	
30 April 1922	6,523	6%	10%	+ 40% bonus
30 April 1923	7,090	6%	12½%	
30 April 1924	3,431	6%	12½%	
30 April 1925	3,269	6%	10%	
30 April 1926	2,537	6%	7½%	
30 April 1927	3,689	6%	10%	
30 April 1928	5,864	6%	15%	
30 April 1929	8,232	6%	20%	
30 April 1930	4,561	6%	12½%	*Vestfos* case settled
30 April 1931	8,808	6%	20%	
30 April 1932	8,861	6%	15%	
30 April 1933	11,475	6%	17½%	
30 April 1934	11,915	6%	20%	
30 April 1935	11,727	6%	20%	
30 April 1936	12,809	6%	20%	
30 April 1937	10,254	6%	20%	Death of Henry Tyrer
30 Sept. 1938	8,450	6%	20%	(17 months period)
31 Aug. 1939	3,699	6%	12½%	(11 months period)
31 Aug. 1940	8,265	6%	15%	
31 Aug. 1941	7,630	6%	10%	
31 Aug. 1942	8,614	6%	15%	
31 Aug. 1943	12,128	6%	20%	
31 Aug. 1944	10,414	6%	20%	
31 Aug. 1945	8,010	6%	30%	Death of Thomas Wilson
31 Aug. 1946	6,683	6%	20%	
31 Aug. 1947	9,128	6%	20%	
31 Aug. 1948	12,688	6%	20%	
31 Aug. 1949	14,218	6%	20%	
31 Aug. 1950	14,551	6%	20%	
31 Aug. 1951	3,918	6%	20%	UAC Agency ended

Table 6 — contd.

Year ending	Net profit[1] £	Preference dividends[2]	Ordinary dividends[2]	Notes
31 Aug. 1952	5,877	6%	25%	
31 Aug. 1953	9,324	6%	25%	
31 Aug. 1954	6,298	6%	25%	
31 Aug. 1955	4,670	6%	25%	Dock strikes
31 Aug. 1956	3,978	6%	25%	
31 Aug. 1957	4,652	6%	25%	
31 Aug. 1958	4,877	6%	25%	
31 Aug. 1959	6,669	6%	25%	
31 Aug. 1960	11,056	6%	25%	
31 Aug. 1961	9,011	6%	25%	
31 Aug. 1962	8.273	6%	25%	
31 Aug. 1963	6,900	6%	25%	
31 Aug. 1964	5,685	6%	25%	
31 Aug. 1965	11,000	6%	25%	
31 Aug. 1966	5,698	6%	25%	
31 Aug. 1967	*1,516 deficit*	6%	15%	Suez crisis & dock strikes
31 Aug. 1968	5,888	6%	17½%	Death of F. Cutts & dock strikes
31 Aug. 1969	3,582	6%	16%	
31 Aug. 1970	5,757	6%	16%	
31 Aug. 1971	18,497	6%	20%	
31 Aug. 1972	17,030	6%	30%	
31 Aug. 1973	16,894	4.2%	49%	

1. 'Net' profit is 'Gross' less depreciation, income tax, profits tax, Directors and Auditors fees and all other expenses.

2. Preference share dividends are free of tax until 1943: Ordinary share dividends are free of tax until 1945. Preference dividends are net after 1973.

Table 7: Exports of Certain Commodities from Nigeria and the Gold Coast, 1899-1951

NIGERIA					
'000 tons	1899-1901	1919-21	1929-31	1935-7	1951
Palm oil	14	80	129	150	150
Palm kernels	52	192	255	346	347
Groundnuts	—	45	151	242	141
Cocoa	—	20	53	91	122
Cotton	—	4	6	11	15
Hides and skins	—	4	6	7	14
Timber	27	29	34	44	394
	93	374	634	891	1,183
GOLD COAST					
Cocoa (000 tons)	1	145	218	272	230
Timber (£000's)	70	123	104	112	4,977

Source: P.T. Bauer, *West African Trade* (London, Cambridge University Press, 1954). Adapted from Table II, p. 195.

West African Imports and Exports

	1936-9 tons	1946-50 tons
Imports		
Nigeria	518,000	785,000
Ghana	469,000	665,000
Gambia	20,000	29,000
Total	1,007,000	1,479,000
Exports		
Nigeria	1,111,000	1,314,000
Ghana	735,000	1,281,000
Gambia	54,000	56,000
Total	1,900,000	2,651,000

Source: *Statistical and Economic Review,* No. XIV (March 1957), p. 18.
Note: This is produced and published by the United Africa Company. The Sierra Leone, and non-British Colonies, also increased in a similar way.

Table 8: Letter in respect of death of Sgt J.E. Lyon

BEF,
France, 26 August 1917

Dear Mrs Lyon,

It is with great regret that I am writing to express my deepest sympathy to you on the loss you have sustained in the death of your husband, Sgt Lyon.

He had only been with me about a month, but this short time had been quite sufficient to prove his worth not only as a soldier but as a leader of men.

He was a most excellent NCO, and was one of the best Sergeants I had ever had the pleasure of commanding. He always worked most industriously and my Company Sergeant Major as well as all the Officers held him in very high esteem.

His death was most unfortunate. It was his first time in action when the Battalion made an attack on July 31st last. The Battalion did magnificently. Your husband had taken command of his Platoon when his Platoon Officer became a casualty, and had successfully led his men to the final objective. They had consolidated the enemy trench they had taken and it was several hours later that he was killed instantly by a German shell. He suffered no pain whatsoever. At the time he was just sitting down in the trench and he could have had no warning of his fate. This may be of some consolation to you, but I fear that it can only be very little.

All his men loved him for he had looked after them so well. His every thought was to look after his men and they appreciated his kindness.

All the Officers, his brother NCO's and men in the Coy. all desire me to convey to you their very deepest sympathy. Our own loss is great but compared to yours it really must be insignificant.

I know you must feel proud of him and you have all reason to be for he was an excellent man and never showed any fear on this his first action and proved himself a hero throughout.

I much regret that owing to being away from the Battalion for some time since the action I have been unable to write to you until now. I beg of you to excuse this delay.

I am, Madam,
Yours in deepest sympathy,
(s) Fred. Atkinson. Capt,
O.C. A Coy. 1/9th K.L.R.

Mrs J.E. Lyon
Ormskirk

Table 9: Ships handled by Tyrer's at Liverpool and Preston

		Liverpool			Preston			
Directors Minute Book no. 1								
Page	Date	Ocean	UAC	Coastwise	Ocean	Coastwise	Dublin	Belfast
105	26 June 1928	64	–	160	–	–	–	–
112	5 July 1929	70	–	153	124	71	56	–
135	21 June 1932	60	22	220	127	81	48	–
141	30 June 1933	62	27	212	146	60	45	–
150	28 June 1934	117	29	200	139	47	46	–
155	3 July 1935	111	28	311	135	46	51	–
161	10 July 1936	107	35	350	130	59	50	–
167	17 Aug. 1937	115	31	319	142	46	62	–
173	23 Nov. 1938	261	48	383	206	93	64	–
177	17 Jan. 1940	144	31	202	127	65	40	–
181	30 Dec. 1940	113	45	197	69	106	18	–
183	12 Mar. 1942	130	–	313	46	258	–	–
188	19 Mar. 1943	138	–	386	20	352	–	–
193	10 Mar. 1944	152	–	379	16	314	–	–
196	20 Feb. 1945	162	–	450	18	385	–	–
202	29 Jan. 1946	227	–	418	27	214	–	–
206	21 Feb. 1947	147	–	380	39	122	–	–
214	31 Aug. 1948	266	–	367	57	57	78	54
225	31 Aug. 1949	281	53	398	84	57	78	123
234	31 Aug. 1950	234	41	343	91	53	58	116
238	31 Aug. 1951	213	–	391	90	52	66	90
240	31 Aug. 1952	231	–	280	90	34	47	77
243	31 Aug. 1953	242	–	382	94	28	52	89
246	31 Aug. 1954	267	–	319	130	25	57	93
249	31 Aug. 1955	241	–	328	130	25	57	63
252	31 Aug. 1956	228	–	284	121	21	54	54
260	31 Aug. 1957	226	–	313	148	18	50	50
Directors Minute Book no. 2								
1	31 Aug. 1958	263	–	257	142	19	50	–
4	31 Aug. 1959	301	–	272	141	9	52	–
6	31 Aug. 1960	334	–	116	171	7	47	(inc. Warren point)
13	31 Aug. 1961	337	–	61	176	7	51	–
21	31 Aug. 1962	303	–	19	149	2	51	*Unit load*
27	31 Aug. 1963	299	–	28	176	2	48	54
34	31 Aug. 1964	327	–	13	213	6	6	48
40	31 Aug. 1965	287	–	7	187	8	–	46
45	31 Aug. 1966	263	–	9	203	2	–	61
49	31 Aug. 1967	242	–	15	194	1	–	–
56	31 Aug. 1968	236	–	10	225	1	–	–
64	31 Aug. 1969	244	–	11	185	5	–	–
75	31 Aug. 1970	256	–	10	133	–	–	–
87	31 Aug. 1971	210	–	–	193	–	–	–
91	31 Aug. 1972	194	–	–	149	–	–	–
97	31 Aug. 1973	216	–	–	143	–	–	–
104	31 Aug. 1974	216	–	–	130	–	–	–

Note: The information above has been obtained from the Directors Minute Books and not every item was always reported. Details of the Southern Whaling and Sealing Company's vessels and of those chartered for the UAC are not included.

Table 10: Directors of Henry Tyrer & Co Ltd, 1914-79

Name	Born	Joined Company	Director	Governing Director	Chairman and Managing Director	Died
Henry Tyrer	1858	1879	1914-36	1914-36		June 36
Thomas Wilson	1883		1914-45	1936-45		May 45
Frederick Cutts	1880	1897	1914-68		1945-68	Oct. 68
James Edward Lyon			1914-17			July 17
Walter Stretch			1914-37			1950
Henry E. Drain		1889	1914-29			1929
Herbert Metcalf Warlow		1897	1914-48			May 48
Harold Cuthbert Lyon			1936-46			1959
George Sanders		1908	1942-63			June 63
Dick Ollerton	1899	1916	1942-60			
John Merriweather			1942-50			Joined Palm Line
James Campbell McNeill			1942-50			Joined Palm Line
Sydney Dalzell		1902	1942-60			Jan. 63
John Pilkington			1942-60			Oct. 77
George Gillen Astbury		1946	1946-50			Joined Palm Line
Charles Wilson Harrison	1918	1935	1956-	V/Chairman 1965-8	1968-	

Table 10 — contd.

Name	Born	Joined Company	Director	Governing Director	Chairman and Managing Director	Died
Thomas E.K. Wilson		1948	1956-65			Sept 65
John Francis Sanders	1929	1951	1956—			
Herbert Barton Warlow		1930	1956-66			Sept. 66
John Lea	1917	1936	1961-..			
James Edward Lyon (Jr)	1917	1933	1961-78	V/Chairman 1968-78		
Rodney Kaye	1924	1953	1965—			
Wilfred Procter Searle	1910	1948	1965-9			Aug 69
George Edmond Stretch	1918	1935	1968			
George Wall	1921	1949	assistant 1968			
David Charles Harrison	1946	1963	assistant 1968 full 1976			
Gordon B. Hannan	1932	1947	assistant 1968 full 1976			

BIBLIOGRAPHY

Original MSS

The papers of Henry Tyrer and of Henry Tyrer and Company Limited, together with those of its associated and subsidiary firms have been catalogued by the author of the present work. They are now filed in 49 'boxes' and are available to responsible persons by application to the Company Secretary at Tyrer's Head Office.

Other primary sources that have been consulted include the papers of the African Steam Ship Company (now held by Ocean Transport and Trading Limited), the records of Heywood's Bank (now kept at Heywood's Branch of Barclay's Bank Limited) and the John Holt archives (which have been deposited with Rhodes House Library in Oxford).

In addition to the details provided by Tyrer's own archives, much information has been obtained from the company returns held at the Companies Registration Office, City Road, London, and at the Public Record Office, Kew. These include:

Becker & Co Ltd
Bromport S.S. Co Ltd
Congo & African Co Ltd
Freight Conveyors Ltd
Henry Tyrer & Co Ltd
Levant Transport Co Ltd
Liver Transport Co Ltd
Minterne s.s. Co Ltd
Port of Chicoutimi Ltd
Preston Steam Navigation Co Ltd
Ribble Coal & Coke Co Ltd
Southern Whaling & Sealing Co Ltd
s.s. Prestonian Ltd
s.s. Prestonian (1902) Ltd
s.s. Princess Ltd
Tyrer Coasters Ltd
Woodpulp Transport Co Ltd

References to these firms are given in the index and in the relevant footnotes.

Government Reports

Committee on Edible and Oil Producing Nuts and Seeds, HMSO, 1916, Cmnd. 8248

Royal Commission on Shipping Rings, HMSO, 1909, Cmnd. 4668-70

Books

Barron, J. *A History of the Ribble Navigation from Preston to the Sea* (Guardian Press, Preston, 1938)

Bauer, P.T. *West African Trade* (Cambridge UP, London, 1954)

Chandler, G. *Liverpool Shipping: A Short History* (Phoenix House, London, 1960)

Davies, P.N. *The Trade Makers. Elder Dempster in West Africa, 1852-1972* (George Allen & Unwin, London, 1973)

_____ (ed) *Trading in West Africa* (Croom Helm, London, 1976)

_____ Sir Alfred Jones, *Shipping Entrepreneur Par Excellence* (Europa, London, 1978)

_____ *A Short History of the Ships of John Holt & Co (Liverpool) Ltd and the Guinea Gulf Line Ltd,* published privately by the Company, Liverpool, 1965

Fayle, C.E. *The War and the Shipping Industry* (Oxford UP, London, 1927)

_____ *Seaborne Trade* (John Murray, London, 1920)

Fry, R. *Bankers in West Africa* (Hutchinson Benham, London, 1976)

Hadfield, C. *British Canals* (Phoenix House, London, 1950)

Hadfield, C. and Biddle, G. *The Canals of North West England* (David and Charles, Newton Abbot, 1970)

Hyde, F.E. *Liverpool and the Mersey* (David and Charles, Newton Abbot, 1971)

_____ *Shipping Enterprise and Management, Harrisons of Liverpool* (Liverpool UP, Liverpool, 1967)

Jackson, G. *The British Whaling Trade* (A. & C. Black, London, 1978)

Kohn, R. *Palm Line: The Coming of Age, 1949-1970,* published privately by the Company, London, 1970

Laird, M. and Oldfield, R.A.K. *Narrative of an Expedition into the interior of Africa by the River Niger . . .* (Richard Bentley, London, 1837)

Lawton, R. *Genesis of Population in Merseyside, A Scientific Survey,* published for the British Association by Liverpool UP, Liverpool, 1953

Lloyd, C. *The Navy and the Slave Trade* (Longmans, London, 1939)

Macgregor, D.R. *The China Bird. The History of Captain Killick and*

100 years of sail and steam (Chatto & Windus, London, 1961)

Mcphee, A. *The Economic Revolution in British West Africa* (George Routledge, London, 1926)

Marriner, S. and Hyde, F.E. *The Senior, John Samuel Swire* (Liverpool UP, Liverpool, 1967)

Marshall, J. *The Lancashire and Yorkshire Railway* (David and Charles, Newton Abbot, 1969)

Mountfield, S. *Western Gateway: A History of the Mersey Docks and Harbour Board* (Liverpool UP, Liverpool, 1965)

Patmore, J.A. and Clarke, J. *Railway History in Pictures: North-west England* (David and Charles, Newton Abbot, 1968)

Plumb and Howard *West African Explorers* (Oxford UP, London, 1955)

Webb, A.N. *An Edition of the Cartulary of Burscough Priory,* printed for the Chetham Society, Manchester UP, Manchester, 1970

Wilson, C. *The History of Unilever,* Book 1 (Cassell, London, 1954)

History of Arthur Heywood, Sons & Co, 1773-1883, published privately by Martins Bank Ltd, Liverpool, 1967

History of the United Africa Company Limited to 1938, produced by the UAC for internal circulation only, London, 1938

Merchant Adventurer published privately by John Holt & Co (Liverpool) Ltd, Liverpool, 1948

Articles

Davies, P.N., 'The African Steam Ship Company', in *Liverpool & Merseyside,* (ed) Harris, J.R. (Frank Cass & Co, London, 1969)
_____ 'The Impact of the Expatriate Shipping Lines on the Economic Development of British West Africa, *Business History,* vol XIX, no. 1, January 1977

Davies, P.N. and Bourn, A.M., 'Lord Kylsant and the Royal Mail', *Business History,* vol XIV, no. 2, July 1972

Drake, B.K., 'Continuity and Flexibility in Liverpool's Trade with Africa and the Caribbean', *Business History,* vol XVIII, no. 1, January 1976

Williams, D.M., 'Abolition and the Re-deployment of the Slave Fleet, 1807-11, *Journal of Transport History,* vol 2, 1973

Works of General Reference

Annual Reports of the Chamber of Shipping
Dictionary of National Biography
Gore's Directories
Handy Shipping Guide

Kelly's Directories
Lloyd's List Law Reports
Lloyd's Register of Shipping
Who Was Who

Periodicals and Newspapers

Fairplay
Financial News
Journal of Commerce
Liverpool Daily Post
Liverpool Echo
Ormskirk Advertiser
Shipping
The Times (see also: Palmer, Samuel, *Index to the Times,* Richmond
    House, Shepperton-on-Thames)

INDEX

Hannan, G.B. 12, 132
Harris, N.C. 13
Harrison, C.W. 11, 12, 13, 95, 96,
    122, 123, 125, 126, 128, 129,
    131, 132, 133, 135 n. 27
Harrison, D.C. 12, 127, 129, 132
Harrison, M. 13, 95, 122
Hartlepool 125
Herlofson, Sigurd 119
Hesketh Bank 27
Hesketh, Sir Thomas George Fermor-
    27, 28
Holland West Africa Line 75,
    79 n. 61, 106, 107
Holmeswood 27
Holt, Alfred and Company 104
Holt, John 18, 37, 39, 40, 42, 43, 44,
    75, 106, 107, 111, 112; John
    Holt Line 112
Hong Kong 118, 126
Hornby, N.A. 61
Hoscar Moss 68
Hothersall, J. (Junior) 13
Hothersall, J. (Senior) 53, 55, 65
Hull 54

India, Shipping Corporation of
    117, 125, 131
India Steam Ship Company 116, 117,
    119, 125, 131
Industrial Revolution 17
Ireland 16, 18, 52, 53, 55, 105, 120
Irvin and Johnson 82
Ishoven, Theo Van 59
Isle of Man 81
Israel 116, 117
Italy 130

Jackson, G. 13
Jaffa Union Line 85
Japan 119
Japp and Kirby 31
Jones, Alfred L. and Company 38
Jones, R.L. 13, 104, 110, 112, 122
Jones, Sir A. 11, 18, 37, 38, 39,
    40, 41, 43, 44, 45, 46
Journal of Commerce 41
Jules, Robin and Company 20

Kaye, R. 12, 126, 127, 132
Ker, Captain W. 45, 46
Killick Martin and Company 131
King John 16
Kings of Bristol 79 n. 54

Kirkcudbright 85
Knott, J. 31, 39, 40
Kortman and Company 59, 60
Kroo boys 46

lager and beer 31
Lagos 46
Lancashire 14, 16, 17, 18, 27, 29,
    125; coal 82
Lancashire Farmers Association 33
Lancashire Paper Mills 54, 55
Lander, R. 36
Laird, H. 37
Laird, M. 36, 37
Laird, W. 37
Lathom 14, 29; charity 28
Lea, J. 12, 132
Leete, W.G. 30
Levant Transport Company Limited
    66
Lever Brothers 11, 71, 72, 73, 74,
    75, 76, 77, 81, 82, 86, 88, 94,
    104, 110; blocked marks 89
Lever's Pacific Plantations 73
Lever, W.H. 11
Leyland Hundred Highway Board 28
Lisbon 117
Liverpool 14-18, 20, 24-30 *passim*,
    50-71 *passim*, 80, 84-91 *passim*,
    96, 103, 108-20 *passim*, 123,
    127, 131, 134
Liverpool and African Steamship
    Shippers Company 42
Liverpool Bankruptcy Court 33
Liverpool Echo 11
Liverpool Grain Storage Company
    Limited 81
Liverpool Steamship Owners
    Association 133
Liver Transport Limited 110, 111,
    113 n. 8, 114 n. 46, 115
Llandulas 124
Llangollen 68
London 17, 18, 30, 36, 37, 41,
    52, 53, 54, 58, 59, 116, 118,
    131; Tyrer's offices 58, 59, 60,
    61, 64, 65, 84, 91
London and India Dock Trust
    Committee 60
Lydiate 29
Lykes Lines 131
Lyon, H.C. 95, 101, 115
Lyon, J.E. (Junior) 12, 95, 96, 125,
    132